COCINA
MEXICANA

FRESH, VIBRANT RECIPES FOR AUTHENTIC MEXICAN FOOD

ADRIANA CAVITA
OF *CAVITA* RESTAURANT, LONDON

PHOTOGRAPHY BY CLARE WINFIELD

RYLAND PETERS & SMALL
LONDON • NEW YORK

DEDICATION

To my homeland, my beloved Mexico. Magic land full of flowers, dances and chants. Land of eagles flying towards the sun.

And to my whole family, especially to my niece Elena and nephew Rodrigo, to remind them that willpower is very important to make their dreams come true and the only thing that can stop them is their own mind/own limits.

Senior designer Megan Smith
Senior editor Abi Waters
Creative director Leslie Harrington
Editorial director Julia Charles
Head of production Patricia Harrington
Editorial consultant Cindy Richards

Food Stylist Rosie Reynolds
Props Stylist Max Robinson
Indexer Vanessa Bird

First published in 2023 by
Ryland Peters & Small
20–21 Jockey's Fields,
London WC1R 4BW
and 341 E 116th Street
New York NY 10029

www.rylandpeters.com

Text © Adriana Cavita 2023
Design and commissioned photographs © Ryland Peters & Small 2023

See page 192 for full picture credits.

ISBN: 978-1-78879-553-1

10 9 8 7 6 5 4 3 2 1

Printed and bound in China

CIP data from the Library of Congress has been applied for. A CIP record for this book is available from the British Library.

NOTES

• Both British (metric) and American (imperial plus US cups) are included; however, it's important not to alternate between the two within a recipe.
• All spoon measurements are level unless specified otherwise.
• All eggs are medium (UK) or large (US), unless specified as large, in which case US extra-large should be used. Uncooked or partially cooked eggs should not be served to the very old, frail, young children, pregnant women or those with compromised immune systems.
• Ovens should be preheated to the specified temperatures. If using a fan-assisted oven, adjust according to the manufacturer's instructions.
• When a recipe calls for the grated zest of citrus fruit, buy unwaxed fruit and wash well before using. If you can only find treated fruit, scrub well in warm soapy water before using.

CONTENTS

INTRODUCTION

The object of this book is to share my love for Mexican cooking through a series of recipes adapted so that they can be easily reproduced at home. Embedded in this objective is also the desire to dismantle some of the stereotypes around Mexican food that still pervade today. For example, not all Mexican food is spicy, nor is everything wrapped in a tortilla, and not every *mole* uses chocolate as an ingredient. Mexico is a country with a complex history and a sophisticated culture, and its cuisine reflects this. Although, on second thoughts, maybe there is some truth in the spicy stereotype...

In 2010, UNESCO declared traditional Mexican cooking an Intangible Cultural Heritage of Humanity, the first time a cooking tradition has been included on this list. A true crucible, influences from all over the world can be traced through Mexican food: Spanish, North African, Middle Eastern, French, Italian, American, even English. We have our own 'Cornish pasties', called *pastes*, prepared in the Mexican state of Hidalgo since the early 19th century. At the same time, native Mexican ingredients have influenced many world cuisines (what would the Italian gastronomy be without tomatoes?).

Underneath this lies a truly ancient way of preparing food unique to Mexico, which also involves the growing and gathering of food. Researching, preserving and continuing this ancient way, still alive in parts of Mexico, is one of my main interests; one that has connected me with my own country, my city, its traditions, and my own family.

I was born in Tlatelolco, a historic neighbourhood in the centre of Mexico City. I do not come from privilege; my parents and grandparents were working class people. My maternal grandfather had a large farm in the state of Tlaxcala, near Mexico City, which we used to visit often. His wife, my grandmother, lived in a different place, Azcapotzalco, now part of the city but then a town of its own. In her garage she ran a little restaurant where her *huaraches* became famous in the neighbourhood. Through this enterprise she was able not only to bring up her seven children and two more she adopted, but she also bought a piece of land and built her own house. Each member of my family (and millions of other hardworking Mexicans) shares a similar story of resilience.

I consider cooking as an art form. Fleeting and ephemeral, like the performance of a play in a theatre; once it is done, it is gone, but the memory can linger. As a child, I was interested in the visual arts, but for reasons too long to explain here, I ended up studying to be a chef (and I am very happy I did). Perhaps this wish to become an artist is what drove me to seek out work with the best chefs that I could find, once I had finished my degree and was a young trainee chef in Mexico City.

From before the Spaniards arrived, Mexico City (my city) was at the centre of a very wide area with many different ecosystems and regions connected. In Tlatelolco, a market city part of the alliance of urban centres around the five lakes in the Valley of Mexico, you could buy fresh fish from the sea and produce from the Yucatán peninsula, many hundred miles away. Like then, Mexico City today is a vibrant and dynamic city where you can taste food from all over the country and even the world, either at small street stalls or in high-end restaurants. The food of Mexico City influences my cooking at my own restaurant in London today.

CAVITA, LONDON

I have been very fortunate to learn from some of the best chefs in the world. In Mexico City I worked with the brilliant Eduardo García from Máximo Bistrot, and then internationally renowned Enrique Olvera from Pujol restaurant, now the ninth best restaurant in the world. In 2011, I worked under the legendary Ferran Adrià as Chef de Partie at El Bulli in Spain. I have also cooked with traditional cooks in small villages across Mexico, and with a very talented chef from Norway in New York City.

After many twists and turns, I was given the chance to open my own restaurant in London. Cavita is where I share my passion for Mexican food with diners. What I do in my restaurant is inevitably the result of all these experiences, but this book is about the basics of Mexican food culture, its vibrant flavours, colours and textures. The recipes here show what Mexicans eat daily, in the streets, in their homes, and when they celebrate with family and friends. I feel a responsibility to preserve my own country's food traditions. I am very grateful to have the opportunity to educate others on Mexican food and its history, while contributing to the history with my own creativity, outside of my own country. I am indebted to all the people who have kept the techniques, ingredients, recipes, utensils and traditions that make up Mexican cuisine; thanks to them, we can all enjoy this multicultural, rich country and its delicious flavours.

THE ORIGINS OF MEXICAN COOKING

Thousands of years ago, somewhere in the hills and plains of Mesoamerica in the centre of Mexico, someone (most probably a woman) had the brilliant idea of using the upright corn/maize plant as a pole to support the climbing bean plant. The corn plant grew stronger and bigger because the bean plant fixes nitrogen in the soil, so she kept sowing them together year after year (first the corn, then a few weeks later, the beans). Then the same ingenious woman, or perhaps her daughters, started to sow plants that creep across the ground, like courgettes/zucchini, between the corn/bean combo, preserving the humidity of the soil and inhibiting weeds, once again benefiting the other two crops.

In North America, some tribes used to call this system of growing three crops together, the Three Sisters, who grow strong when they are together. In Mexico, where the system was first developed, it is called the *milpa* system. *Milpa* is a Nahuatl word that simply means 'kitchen garden' or 'vegetable patch'. (Nahuatl is one of the main native languages of Central Mexico, and the one the Aztecs spoke; today there are about 1½ million speakers of Nahuatl.) This productive way of cultivating small patches of land spread to northeast North America all the way down to Central America, and today is still used in rural areas from Central Mexico down to Guatemala and Honduras.

Those three crops are also grown alongside with a wide variety of herbs and vegetables, some for medicine, others for food, like potatoes, chilli/chile peppers, tomatoes and amaranth. Professor H. Garrison Wilkes, a food historian and researcher at the University of Massachusetts in Boston, considers the *milpa* as 'one of the most successful human inventions ever created'.

In Mexico there was a second very successful invention: the nixtamalization of corn (see page 26). Again, nixtamal is a composite Nahuatl word. 'Nix' means 'ashes', and 'tamalli' refers to cooked corn dough. The earliest evidence we have of this process dates from 1200–1500 BC. Archaeologists tell us that people used to heat water for cooking by placing hot stones inside the pots, which can explain the presence of lime in the pots used to cook corn.

I like the idea that, perhaps, it was all a kitchen accident: some ashes (containing lime) ended up in the pot where the dry corn kernels were cooking, and then the woman realized that the ash had made the corn softer, easier to crush, and that the dough resulting from it could be moulded into flat circles without crumbling. The dough was malleable yet strong, a bit like clay. When cooked, she found these first tortillas were not only delicious, but also pliable and strong enough to hold other foods.

What she probably didn't know at that moment is that the lime had also enhanced the nutritional value of the corn, releasing substances like amino acids and proteins, making them available to humans. It is not too much to say that this other 'successful human invention' helped the peoples of Mesoamerica to create the great urban civilizations that came later.

Corn was first domesticated in Mexico, but as you probably know already, the list of crops that our ancestors developed across this continent is quite long: tomatoes, cacao, vanilla, some types of beans, squash, sunflowers, papayas, peppers, avocado, pineapple, peanuts, and from South America we have potatoes (a great contribution from the Incas to the world) and quinoa.

TRADITIONAL COOKING METHODS & TOOLS

NIXTAMAL

Corn/maize is the foundation of all Mexican cooking. It is like bread for Europeans: the one thing you eat every day with almost every meal (unless you are on a low-carb diet). As with bread, nixtamalized corn dough can be transformed into many different shapes, and it can be savoury or sweet.

The most delicious homemade tortillas are the ones made following the same principles used for millennia in Mexico. As the saying goes, 'if it ain't broke, don't fix it'. People still make tortillas in this way in small villages, and now this method of making tortillas is coming back to urban centres.

It all starts the day before, boiling the dry corn kernels with a pinch or two of lime, and then leaving them to soak. Variations on the boiling and soaking times give different results, so for example, in Oaxaca, to make those large tortillas called *tlayudas* (see page 97), women shorten the boiling and soaking times, so the kernels are more al dente, and this results in a dough that can be made into thinner and larger tortillas.

After the boiling and soaking, the kernels need to be milled or ground. The resulting dough can be used right away to make tortillas or tamales, or it can be dried to make flour. This corn/maize flour can now be bought online. By adding water, the flour rehydrates and can be used to make tortillas. But if you ever travel to Mexico and are lucky to taste a fresh tortilla made with last night's nixtamal, you will understand why Mexicans still make it this way.

METATE & MOLCAJETE

The grinding of the nixtamal corn is hard work. Before mechanical mills, people used a beautiful tool called a *metate*. Normally a stone, the tool

is softly curved to accommodate the corn kernels to be ground with another soft, cylindrical stone. Some *metates* are big, others small; most of them have little legs to elevate the work surface. When you visit Mexico, you will see them in ethnographic museums, and if you travel to villages and small communities, you may see them in action.

They say the dough made with a *metate* will have a better texture and flavour. Perhaps the volcanic stones used to make *metates* passes on some of its minerals to the dough. Who knows? The fact is that *metates* are still used in many places in Mexico. They don't require electricity, and they connect people with their ancestors.

The other ubiquitous tool in Mexican cooking is the *molcajete*, which is a mortar, but generally bigger and made with volcanic basalt. If *metates* are almost exclusively used to grind corn, in a *molcajete* you can grind anything: tomatoes, chillies/chiles, seeds, herbs and spices. It does the job of an electric blender, sauces made in a *molcajete* will have a slightly different texture and perhaps flavour than those made with an electric blender. You can now buy *molcajetes* outside of Mexico and try your hand at it with the salsas in the 'Basics' chapter.

COMAL

Another very useful tool in the Mexican kitchen is the *comal* (the name is also derived from the Nahuatl word *comalli*). They are big, round, flat pans with no sides, traditionally made from clay, but nowadays you can buy metallic ones in any market. The clay *comal* must be 'cured' with water and lime before being used for the first time, then it can be placed directly over an open flame, either from a wood fire or a gas stove.

Mexicans use *comales* to cook tortillas, as well as the *quesadillas* and *itacates* found in the 'Street Food' chapter. You don't need a *comal* to make tortillas, you can use any good frying pan/skillet or, better yet, a crêpe pan as I mention in the tortilla recipe (see page 26).

We also use it a lot to toast ingredients used in sauces like tomatoes, chillies/chiles, seeds, onions and garlic. Although the dictionary will tell you *asar* means 'to roast' or 'to grill', I would say that in Mexico this term means 'to toast', like when you toast pumpkin seeds before tossing them into a salad, to release their oils and flavours.

A *comal* is a very simple, beautiful thing, that can be used to make quite complex dishes. With a large enough one, women can cook almost anything. The surface of the *comal* will be at different temperatures at the same time, so you can use this to your advantage. You can cook simultaneously something very fast and keep other ingredients on the lower heat, and keep yet other elements warm. You can even dry chillies when the fire is out, making the most of the fire's energy.

MEXICAN INGREDIENTS

Charles de Gaulle complained about how difficult it was to govern a nation with more than 300 types of cheese. The same can be said of Mexico and its chiles. The only common trait of this diversity is this: when you ask a Mexican if something is spicy, he or she will say "no".
JUAN VILLORO, from his essay 'Dramáticos Placeres: el chile mexicano', in *Safari Accidental* (2005)

You may have noticed just how many words come from Nahuatl, like *comal* and *nixtamal*. But perhaps you will be surprised to hear that *chocolate* and *tomate* also come from it. The word 'Mexico' in Nahuatl means 'the bellybutton of the moon'.

It could be said that Mexico really is a kind of bellybutton, situated in the centre of a continent, and in between Europe and Asia. Its position on the planet has afforded Mexico a great variety of ingredients and ways to prepare them, making the Mexican kitchen literally a melting pot of cultures. Not too long after the first Europeans arrived in Mexico and Central America, they found their way to India from the Pacific coast. The trade routes with Asia were established, and the interchange of food made Mexico one of the richest places on earth gastronomically speaking.

Europeans brought their animals with them and, of course, their crops, but they also protected others. (It was prohibited to grow grapes for wine in the Americas, although some people did it; the history of wine in our continent is fascinating.)

Mango and tamarind trees arrived in Mexico from Asia, and all the different spices, like black pepper and cinnamon, became staple ingredients n Mexican cooking. In return, we sent the chillies to Asia, where they quickly became part of the diet, especially in the southern regions like India, Thailand and Indonesia. Everywhere in the world Mexican and American plants adapted and grew into many different varieties.

Super healthy avocados, full of good fat, are a staple of Mexican diet. As mentioned above, they are a native tree, with a funny anecdote about their name: the word *aguacate* in Nahuatl means 'the

testicle of a tree'. The leaves of the avocado tree can be used in the kitchen too; I use them a lot. They have a subtle flavour, a bit like laurel (both trees are related). In the UK, you can buy them dried, or even dried and made into a powder. Avocado leaves also make a medicinal tea used in Mexico for many different ailments. Alternatively, you can plant an avocado stone and grow your own tree. Even if the little thing never gives you avocados, you can still use the leaves!

There is another super healthy food in the basic Mexican diet: the young, tender leaves of the prickly pear cactus, called *nopal* in Mexico. These you can grill, fry or boil, and they are usually served chopped with tomatoes, onion, fresh chillies/chiles, and coriander/cilantro. You can even eat them raw, blended in your morning smoothie, but they are an acquired taste. Mexicans eat a lot of mushrooms. When you travel to small villages in the mountains, you will find people selling wild mushrooms in the markets. In fact, in Mexico people still regularly forage for food in forests, like the *tecojotes* used in the Hot Fruit Punch on page 163; they pick up medicinal herbs and tree barks, berries, mushrooms, flowers, insects and worms as well as wild vegetables.

I could go on and on; the list is endless... But the good news is that you can buy the basics from specialist retailers online and increasingly in your local supermarket. In the recipes that follow, I have given substitutes for ingredients that are trickier to source. Once you start making these recipes, you will find they are very easy to adapt and experiment with. I hope this book helps you to incorporate some of my country's ways of cooking, flavours and textures into your own kitchen.

BASIC RECIPES
PREPARACIONES BASICAS

BASIC RAW SALSAS
SALSA CRUDA BASICAS

*The following raw salsa recipes are the most common basic recipes
to make at home. They are very good accompaniments for tacos, tostadas,
main dishes or they can be used as dips.*

TOMATILLO SALSA

SALSA DE TOMATILLO

*A very common salsa in Mexico
and perfect for adding freshness
to a dish when you're in a hurry.*

10 tomatillos, husks removed,
   skins peeled (see Note below),
   washed and halved
¼ small onion, cut in half
2 small garlic cloves
1 or 2 fresh jalapeños, stems
   removed, cut into 3 pieces
4 tablespoons olive oil
1 tablespoon salt
20 g/½ cup roughly chopped
   fresh coriander/cilantro

MAKES ABOUT 700 G/3 CUPS

Put all the ingredients in a
blender and blend until mixed
and roughly chopped. Blend for
longer if you prefer a smoother
salsa. Taste and add more salt if
needed. Transfer to a bowl and
serve the same day preferably, or
store in an airtight container in
the fridge and use within 3 days.

*Note To peel the tomatillos,
soak them in a bowl of just
boiled water for 5 minutes, cut
a shallow cross in the top of
each one, then carefully peel
the skins away.*

HABENERO SALSA

SALSA DE HABANERO

*This salsa is common in the
Yucatán peninsula. It is very
lightly spiced, but you can leave
in the chilli seeds if preferred.*

12 tomatoes, asados
   (see Note below), skins peeled
¼ small onion, asada
1 garlic clove, asado
1 or 2 fresh habanero or 1 Scotch
   bonnet chilli/chile, asado, seeds
   removed (or seeds left in if you
   like more of a kick)
½ tablespoon dried Mexican
   oregano
½ tablespoon salt

MAKES ABOUT 1 LITRE/4 CUPS

Put all the ingredients in a
blender with 120 ml/½ cup
water and blend until smooth.
Alternatively, pulse together for
a rougher 'molcajete-style' sauce
(see page 188). Taste and adjust
the seasoning if needed. Store
in an airtight container in the
fridge and use within 3 days.

*Note Asado or asada means
that a vegetable has been
cooked over hot coals or in a
hot pan before use. See page
188 for a full explanation.*

MEXICAN SALSA

SALSA MEXICANA

*A common salsa used all over
Mexico enjoyed as a snack
with tostadas (see page 29) or
totopos (crunchy fried tortillas).*

4 tomatoes, seeds removed
   and flesh finely diced
½ small onion, finely diced
1 or 2 fresh jalapeños, 2 green
   Thai chillies/chiles, or any fresh
   green chilli/chile you can find,
   finely diced
20 g/½ cup roughly chopped
   fresh coriander/cilantro
1 tablespoon salt
juice of 1½ limes
2 tablespoons olive oil

MAKES ABOUT 500 G/2 CUPS

Put all the ingredients in a bowl
and stir to combine. Taste and
add more salt if needed. Store
in an airtight container in the
fridge and use within 3 days.

*Note This makes a very good
dip and can also be used as the
base for guacamole – just add
the smashed flesh of 2 avocados
and some more lime juice and
salt to taste.*

AVOCADO SALSA

GUACASALSA

This is one of the creamiest and tastiest salsas. It is so versatile and speedy to prepare, making it a perfect accompaniment for most dishes.

5 avocados, stoned/pitted and
　peeled
bunch of fresh coriander/cilantro,
　roughly chopped
5 jalapeños, stems removed
　and cut into 3 pieces
120 ml/½ cup lime juice
1 tablespoon salt
120 ml/½ cup olive oil

MAKES ABOUT 700 G/3 CUPS

Put all the ingredients in a blender with 120 ml/½ cup water and mix to a smooth texture. Alternatively, use a handheld stick/immersion blender. Taste and add more salt if needed. Store in an airtight container in the fridge and use within 3 days.

Note You can also pass the salsa through a fine-mesh sieve/strainer for an even smoother finish.

CITRUS & TOMATO SALSA

SALSA XNIPEK

This is a well-known sauce from the Yucatán region. Traditionally, people use a very acidic local orange to prepare it, but here I have altered the ingredients slightly to get as close to the flavour as possible.

4–6 tomatoes, seeds removed
　and flesh finely diced
½ red onion, thinly sliced
¼ or ½ cup habanero or Scotch
　bonnet chillies/chiles, seeds and
　veins removed, thinly sliced
120 ml/½ cup orange juice
1 tablespoon white wine vinegar
1 tablespoon salt

MAKES ABOUT 500 G/2 CUPS

Put all the ingredients in a bowl and stir to combine. Taste and add more salt if needed. Leave to rest for about 30 minutes. Mix again before serving. Store in an airtight container in the fridge and use within 3 days.

Note I sometimes like to add 2 tablespoons olive oil to make the salsa a bit more shiny.

BASIC COOKED SAUCES
SALSAS COCIDAS BASICAS

These cooked sauces are used in many of my recipes. It is a good idea to make them in batches so that you have plenty on hand for serving with dishes.

GREEN SAUCE
SALSA DE TOMATILLOS ASADOS

This is one of my favourite sauces, particularly when it is made over hot coals in the traditional way to create a smoky flavour (see Variation).

14 tomatillos, husks removed, skins peeled (see page 19) and washed
½ small onion
1 garlic clove
1 or 2 fresh jalapeños, stems removed and cut into 3 pieces
2 tablespoons olive oil
1 tablespoon salt
20 g/½ cup finely chopped fresh coriander/cilantro (or pinch of cumin seeds)

MAKES ABOUT 400–500 G/ 1½–2 CUPS

Heat a heavy-based frying pan/ skillet or comal over a medium heat. Add the garlic and cook, turning frequently, until soft and lightly charred all over. Remove the garlic and set aside. Turn the heat up to medium–high, add the tomatillos and onion and cook until slightly charred all over. The trick is to turn the tomatillos every 2 minutes, otherwise you will end up with a tomatillo purée.

Transfer the cooked vegetables to a food processor or blender, along with the jalapeños, oil and salt and blend until mixed. Alternatively, use a handheld/ stick immersion blender. If you are using cumin seeds instead of coriander, add these to the blender too. Transfer to a bowl, taste and add more salt if needed. Stir through the coriander to finish. Serve the same day preferably or store in an airtight container in the fridge and use within 3 days.

VARIATION You can use a more authentic method to make this salsa It takes a bit more time, but is worth it. To 'asar' the vegetables and jalapeños, they will need to be cooked over hot coals until they are lightly charred all over. Crush the cumin seeds in a molcajete (see page 188) or a large mortar. Add the charred garlic and smash and crush to a paste. Add the charred onion, tomatillos and jalapeños and mix together in the molcajete. Season with salt to taste.

RED SAUCE
SALSA DE JITOMATE COCIDA

Another basic sauce made in Mexican homes, usually with jalapeños, but any fresh chilli/ chile will work.

8 tomatoes, skins peeled and washed
¼ small onion
1 garlic clove
1 or 2 fresh jalapeños, 2 morita chillies/chiles or your favourite chilli/chile, seeds removed (or seeds left in, if you like more of a kick)
20 g/½ cup roughly chopped fresh coriander/cilantro
1 tablespoon salt

MAKES ABOUT 1 LITRE/4 CUPS

Put all the ingredients in a saucepan with 480 ml/2 cups water and cook over a medium– high heat for 15–20 minutes. Leave to cool down slightly. Transfer to a blender and blend to a smooth sauce. Alternatively, use a handheld stick/immersion blender. Store in an airtight container in the fridge and use within 3 days.

Note Pass the sauce through a fine-mesh sieve/strainer for an even smoother finish, if liked.

TORTILLAS

TORTILLAS

In the past, tortillas were shaped by hand, without a tortilla press. My grandma used to make them like that, and in some small communities women still shape their tortillas in this way. If you are using a tortilla press, you will need a really thin sheet of plastic, like the kind used by a butcher when weighing out meat. In Mexico, women recycle thin plastic bags from the corner shop. They wash, disinfect and dry the bags with a towel before cutting them to the size of the tortilla press. The number of tortillas the recipe makes will depend on the size you shape them – they could be small (30 g/1 oz. each), medium (60 g/2 oz. each) or large (90 g/3 oz. each). They can be any size really, but that may be dependent on the size of your tortilla press.

NIXTAMAL
1 kg/2¼ lb. dried corn kernels
(maize)
2 litres/8 cups water
10–15 g/2–3 teaspoons calcium
hydroxide (see Note on page 28)

NIXTAMALIZED CORN DOUGH
1 kg/2¼ lb. Nixtamal (see above)
or nixtamalized corn flour
1 tablespoon table salt (optional)

metallic hand mill
tortilla press
2 thin sheets of plastic

**MAKES ABOUT 30 SMALL,
15 MEDIUM OR 10 LARGE
TORTILLAS**

To make the nixtamal, place all the ingredients in a large saucepan over a medium heat and bring to the boil. Cook for about 5 minutes, or until al dente. Remove from the heat and leave to rest overnight.

Rinse the nixtamalized corn in a sieve/strainer with cold running water to remove as much of the skins as possible.

Pass the rinsed corn through a metallic hand mill to make a smooth paste. You may need to pass it through the mill twice to achieve the right consistency. The soaked corn is partially rehydrated and will already look like dough once milled. I add a little water when I'm milling, but be careful not to add too much water otherwise it won't be easy to shape the tortillas. The dough shouldn't be too sticky.

If you are using nixtamalized corn flour instead of nixtamal, rehydrate the corn flour by gradually adding warm water (about a cup of water for every cup of flour) until it forms into a dough.

On a clean surface, work the nixtamalized corn dough to a smooth texture. Knead the salt into the dough, if using. The dough shouldn't stick to your hands easily and should have a clay-like texture.

Divide the dough into equal portions according to the size of tortillas you want to make. When not in use, always cover the portioned dough with a damp dish towel to stop them drying out and becoming too hard to use.

Preheat a large frying pan/skillet over a high heat – ideally you want to use one with very low sides, almost like a crêpe pan.

Before you start to make the tortillas, make sure you have a place to put them once they are ready. In Mexico, we have special baskets

Notes

The quantity of calcium hydroxide needed depends on its quality. The only way to know exactly how much you need to use is to adjust the quantity each time you make tortillas and settle on the amount that works best for you – 15 g/½ oz. is the amount that I generally use.

If you want to keep the tortillas for use the next day, I recommend wrapping them in a clean, dry dish towel and placing them inside a plastic bag so they don't dry out.

I sometimes use fried tortillas as a garnish. Cut the tortillas into thin strips, heat 240 ml/1 cup vegetable oil in a saucepan and fry the tortilla strips. Place them on kitchen paper to absorb any excess oil.

and use a clean, dry dish towel to cover them until needed. If you don't have a basket, a medium-sized bowl or plate will work just as well.

Place 2 thin sheets of plastic inside the tortilla press. Shape one of the portions of dough into a ball. Work and roll the dough into a perfectly round ball for best results. Place it in between the plastic in the tortilla press and close – do not press too hard, but also not too soft. The tortilla should be about 3–4 mm/⅛ inches thick.

Place the tortilla in the hot, dry pan over a medium–high heat. Cook for about 20 seconds, turn, and then cook for a further 60–90 seconds. Turn and cook again for another 20 seconds. It is a quick process, but if you follow the cooking times, your tortilla should puff up. It takes practice. Continue until you have used up all the dough.

Either serve the tortillas right away or warm them up again before serving by putting them in a dry pan over a medium–high heat for 20–30 seconds on each side. The tortillas should be used within 3 days or can be frozen for up to 6 months.

TOSTADAS
TOSTADAS

Tostadas are a crunchy version of a tortilla and are basically an already cooked tortilla that is then fried in oil. For best results, use thinly pressed tortillas that are a day or two old for making tostadas.

1 litre/4 cups vegetable oil
10 cooked tortillas
   (see page 26)

SERVES 4–6

Add the oil to a large frying pan/skillet with deep sides and heat to 170°C/325°F on a cooking thermometer. Fry the tortillas, one by one, to a golden colour. The trick is to flip each tortilla in the oil from one side to the other very quickly to avoid them puffing up.

VARIATION You can also make tostadas in an oven preheated to 180°C/ 160°C fan/350°F/Gas 4. Line a large baking sheet with non-stick parchment paper and spray or brush the paper with oil. Lay the tortillas on the oiled paper; space them apart so they are not touching, otherwise they will stick together. Add a bit more oil all over and lay another sheet of parchment paper over the top. Top with another baking sheet to keep the tortillas flat. Cook for about 25–30 minutes, depending on how thick they are, until they take on a bit of colour and are crunchy in texture. Alternatively, they can also be cooked slowly over a hot grill for about 1 hour until crunchy.

RICE

ARROZ

There are many different ways to prepare rice in Mexico, but these are probably the simplest and tastiest methods.

WHITE RICE

ARROZ BLANCO

60 ml/¼ cup vegetable oil
180 g/1 cup basmati rice, rinsed and dried as well as possible
¼ onion, finely chopped
2 garlic cloves, finely chopped
70 g/½ cup peeled and cubed potatoes
60 g/½ cup peeled and cubed carrots
75 g/½ cup peas
1 tablespoon salt

SERVES 2

Place the oil and rice in a saucepan over a medium heat and cook, stirring continuously to prevent the rice sticking, for about 5 minutes. Add the onion and garlic and stir through.

Once the rice starts to make some noise – when the rice starts to 'sing', as we say – add the potatoes and carrots and cook for 2 minutes. Finally, add 480 ml/2 cups water and the peas and salt. Cover with a lid and simmer for 15–20 minutes.

GREEN RICE

ARROZ VERDE

60 ml/¼ cup vegetable oil
180 g/1 cup basmati rice, rinsed and dried as well as possible
30 g/½ cup fresh parsley
20 g/½ cup fresh coriander/ cilantro
¼ onion, roughly chopped
2 garlic cloves
360 ml/1½ cups chicken or vegetable stock or water
150 g/1 cup peas (optional)
1 tablespoon salt

SERVES 2

Place the oil and rice in a saucepan over a medium heat and cook, stirring continuously to prevent the rice sticking, for about 5 minutes.

Meanwhile, blend the herbs, onion and garlic in a food processor. Measure out 480 ml/ 2 cups of this mixture, adding some of the stock or water to make up the difference if needed.

Once the rice starts to make some noise – when the rice starts to 'sing', as we say – add the herb mixture, remaining stock or water, peas, if using, and salt. Bring to the boil, taste and adjust the seasoning if needed. Cover with a lid and simmer for 15–20 minutes.

RED RICE

ARROZ ROJO

60 ml/¼ cup vegetable oil
180 g/1 cup basmati rice, rinsed and dried as well as possible
4 tomatoes, roughly chopped
¼ onion, roughly chopped
2 garlic cloves
240 ml/1 cup stock or water
70 g/½ cup peeled and cubed potatoes
60 g/½ cup peeled and cubed carrots
75 g/½ cup peas
1 tablespoon salt
2 fresh parsley sprigs

SERVES 2

Place the oil and rice in a saucepan over a medium heat and cook, stirring continuously, for about 5 minutes. Meanwhile, blend the tomatoes, onion and garlic in a food processor. Measure out 240 ml/1 cup of this mixture, adding some of the stock to make up the difference if needed. Once the rice starts to make some noise, add the potatoes and carrots and cook for 2 minutes. Add the tomato mixture, remaining stock or water, peas and salt. Mix carefully. Once it has changed colour to a more intense red, add another 240 ml/1 cup water and the parsley. Cover with a lid and simmer for 15–20 minutes.

POT BEANS

FRIJOLES DE LA OLLA

This is the most popular and simplest way to prepare beans, which are often used as a base for other recipes. These delicious beans can also be served with any breakfast or as a side with main dishes.

250 g/9 oz. dried beans
  (see Note opposite)
½ white onion, peeled and
  left whole
4 garlic cloves, peeled and
  left whole
1 tablespoon salt
1 tablespoon dried hoja santa
  or a bunch of fresh coriander/
  cilantro

SERVES 4

Soak the beans in a bowl of water overnight. The next day, drain the beans and cook in a saucepan with the rest of the ingredients following the packet instructions until they are soft. Taste and add more salt if needed. Store in an airtight container in the fridge and use within 3 days.

Note *There are over 70 varieties of beans in Mexico, and any will work with this recipe. Use your favourite kind or experiment with different varieties to find the best flavour to suit your taste.*

BREAKFASTS
DESAYUNO

The variety of food we eat for breakfast in Mexico is mind-blowing. It is one of the most popular meals of the day. As Mexicans always have a late lunch, a substantial breakfast is vital in order to keep energy levels up during the day.

In the larger Mexican cities, people often meet for breakfast. It is a meal that can be shared with friends and work colleagues, but unlike lunch, there is no risk of not making it back to the office afterwards. These are elaborate breakfasts with several courses: first, coffee and juice with pastries or slices of papaya, mango, melon and watermelon, then follows a hot dish with eggs, pork or chicken, or in the north of Mexico, with dried beef. (Mexicans also love French toast, waffles and pancakes.)

Freshly squeezed orange juice vendors abound on the street corners of cities and towns. Small stalls are equipped with several blenders and juicers, where you can buy in a hurry the most amazing smoothies made with all kinds of fruits and cereals, like amaranth or oats. Traditional Mexican breakfast drinks also include *café de olla* (see page 168), coffee made in a big pot with cinnamon and sugar, or the pre-Hispanic *atole*, a thick, creamy beverage made with corn flour, served hot and in many different flavours (cinnamon, chocolate and fruits to name just a few).

In small towns around Mexico, women still wake up before sunrise to grind their *nixtamal*, the corn dough that forms the base of their diet (see page 26). Then, after shaping the dough into flat, round tortillas, they will cook them in the *comal*, a big round clay or metal dish that is placed directly on top of a flame. If cooked over a wood fire, tortillas will have a distinctive, smoky flavour.

These tortillas can then be eaten with eggs cooked in many ways: fried eggs sat on top of lightly fried tortillas, topped with salsa and with a side of black beans, or scrambled eggs with chillies/chiles, tomatoes and onions and eaten as tacos with a dollop of salsa and a slice of avocado. These last ones, called simply *huevos a la Mexicana* or Mexican-style eggs, are my favourite breakfast (see page 46), I serve them with tortillas and a steamy, sweet cup of *café de olla*.

Tortillas can also be used in more elaborate breakfast dishes like *enchiladas* (see page 45), where they are bathed in a red tomato sauce or green tomatillo sauce, filled with shredded chicken and topped with crumbly fresh cheese. Or there are the famous *enfrijoladas* that are similar to *enchiladas*, but instead of red or green sauce the tortillas are dunked in *frijoles de la olla* (see page 32).

However, one of the most popular breakfast dishes in Mexico, *chilaquiles* (see page 42), is made with 'yesterday's' tortillas. These are cut into small pieces called *totopos*, fried until crisp, and then covered with green or red sauce and topped with fried eggs or shredded chicken, a dollop of sour cream and a few slices of red onion. *Chilaquiles* are related to the nachos served in any cinema/movie theater around the globe today, but like distant cousins, they would not recognize each other if they met in the flesh.

As a last note, I must mention the way Mexicans 'cure' a bad hangover: with a good *caldo* (broth) for breakfast. This broth can be made with chicken, beef, pork or prawns/shrimp, but is always very spicy and warming. Served with a beer mixed with lemon juice and a bit of salt, nothing beats a hangover like a *caldo*. There are restaurants in Mexico City that serve only *caldos*, and on any given Sunday, there you will find all the night birds trying to become human again. For a classic hangover cure, try the *Caldo Tlalpeño* (see page 118).

(From top left clockwise) A beautiful display of heirloom corn in Tlaxcala; cooking fresh new corn in September with the Wixárika nation; a colourful fresh fruit stall in Chiapas; two women chatting and cleaning beans; woman serving atole in a town called Ixcatlán, Oaxaca.

FARMER'S EGGS
HUEVOS RANCHEROS

This is one of the most popular Mexican breakfasts all over the world and can usually be found in any Mexican restaurant serving breakfast. The tostada (crunchy fried tortilla) on the bottom and saucy egg on top definitely makes it a very tasty and unique dish.

250 ml/1 cup vegetable oil
4 tortillas (see page 26)
500 ml/2 cups Red Sauce
  (see page 25)
500 ml/2 cups Green Sauce
  (see page 25)
4 eggs
sea salt

TO SERVE
Pot Beans (see page 32), warmed
grated/shredded cheese
  (your favourite kind) (optional)
chopped fresh coriander/cilantro

SERVES 2

Add the oil to a frying pan/skillet over a medium heat and fry the tortillas – they should be crunchy but not too crunchy. Transfer them to a bowl lined with kitchen paper to absorb any excess oil.

Meanwhile, gently warm up the red and green sauces in separate saucepans. The sauces need to be runny – if they are a bit dry, add a little water, chicken stock or vegetable stock if necessary. Taste and adjust the seasoning if needed.

In the same pan you used to cook the tortillas fry the eggs over a medium heat until they are cooked to your liking.

Place 2 tortillas on each plate, side by side. Add a serving spoonful of the red sauce to one of the tortillas and of the green sauce to the other. Arrange 2 fried eggs on top and spoon the beans on the side of the eggs.

Add some grated cheese on top, if using (this is optional, but I recommend it), and some chopped coriander leaves before serving.

SCRAMBLED EGGS WITH GREEN BEANS

HUEVOS CON EJOTES

This is probably one of the less well known Mexican breakfast recipes. It is usually enjoyed in rural areas during the summer months when green beans are in season.

2 tablespoons butter or vegetable oil
120 g/½ cup thinly sliced onions
200 g/7 oz. green beans, each cut into 3 pieces
4 eggs
½ teaspoon sea salt
½ teaspoon freshly ground black pepper
warm tortillas (see page 26), to serve

SERVES 2

Place the butter or oil in a frying pan/skillet over a medium heat. Add the onion and cook for about 5 minutes or until they are translucent. Add the green beans with a pinch of salt and cook for 2 minutes.

Meanwhile, crack the eggs into a bowl, add the salt and pepper and beat vigorously with a fork. Add the beaten eggs to the pan and cook, stirring continuously to keep the eggs moving, until they are cooked to your liking.

Serve the scrambled eggs and green beans immediately with freshly warmed tortillas.

BUILDER'S EGGS

HUEVOS AL ALBAÑIL

Making these quick, delicious and saucy scrambled eggs is a great way to use up any leftover Mexican sauces you may have in the fridge.

4 eggs
1 teaspoon salt
½ teaspoon freshly ground black pepper
2 tablespoons butter or vegetable oil
500 ml/2 cups Red Sauce (see page 25)

TO SERVE
50 g/½ cup grated/shredded cheese (your favourite type)
Pot Beans (see page 32), warmed
warm tortillas (see page 26)

SERVES 2

Crack the eggs into a bowl, add the salt and pepper and beat vigorously with a fork.

Place the butter or oil in a saucepan over a medium heat. Add the beaten eggs to the pan and cook, stirring continuously to keep the eggs moving, until they are cooked to your liking.

Meanwhile, heat the red sauce in a separate pan. Once the sauce is bubbling, add the scrambled eggs and gently stir them in until everything is mixed together. Taste and adjust the seasoning if needed.

Place 2 tortillas on each plate, side by side. Divide the saucy scrambled eggs between the plates, then top with beans and add some grated cheese on top if liked.

CHILAQUILES

CHILAQUILES

This is one of the most traditional breakfasts in Mexico. Usually we add epazote, a Mexican herb, but as it is very difficult to find outside of Mexico, you can use hoja santa powder or fresh coriander/cilantro instead.

1 litre/4 cups rapeseed oil,
   for frying
30 tortillas (see page 26),
   cut into triangles

SAUCE
8–10 dried morita chillies/chiles,
   seeds and veins removed
1 kg/2¼ lb. ripe tomatoes, asados
   (see Note below)
½ large white onion, asada
5 garlic cloves, asado
1 tablespoon sea salt
150 ml/⅔ cup olive oil
1 litre/4 cups chicken or vegetable
   stock
small bunch of fresh coriander/
   cilantro, chopped

TO SERVE
250 g/1 cup sour cream
300 g/10½ oz. feta cheese
   (or use Parmesan for a stronger
   flavour)
½ red onion, thinly sliced
1 avocado, stoned/pitted, peeled
   and roughly chopped
40 g/1 cup chopped fresh
   coriander/cilantro (or 1 teaspoon
   hoja santa powder)

SERVES 6

First, make the sauce. Put the dried chillies in a bowl of warm water and leave to soak for 20 minutes. Drain and discard the soaking water (or reserve the soaking liquid and use to loosen the sauce when it is blended if you like more spice).

Add the asados vegetables to a food processor with the soaked chillies and salt, then blend together until combined. Strain through a fine-mesh sieve/strainer to create a smoother mixture if liked.

Heat the olive oil in a saucepan over a medium heat, then add the strained sauce and cook for about 10 minutes. Add the stock (or chilli soaking water) and coriander and cook for about 15 minutes. Taste and adjust the seasoning. Keep the sauce simmering over a low heat while you cook the tortillas. The sauce needs to be quite liquid, otherwise the chilaquiles will be too dry – you can add more of the chilli soaking water if needed.

Preheat the oil in a deep saucepan to 170°C/325°F on a cooking thermometer. Deep-fry the tortillas in the hot oil for 4–5 minutes or until crisp and golden. Place the fried tortillas (*totopos*) on a baking sheet lined with kitchen paper to absorb any excess oil.

Increase the heat under the sauce – it needs to be very hot when you add the *totopos*. Add the *totopos* to the sauce and gently mix everything together.

As soon as the totopos are well coated, immediately pour the chilaquiles onto a serving platter – you need to do this quickly and then serve them straight away in order to enjoy the chilaquiles while they are still crunchy. Top the chilaquiles with the sour cream, feta, red onion, avocado and coriander.

Note Asado or asada means that a vegetable has been cooked over hot coals or in a hot pan before use. See page 188 for a full explanation.

CHICKEN ENCHILADAS
ENCHILADAS ROJAS

Enchiladas are a bit messy to prepare, but once they are made you won't regret it. Feel free to increase the number of tortillas depending on how hungry you are.

1 litre/4 cups Red Sauce
   (see page 25)
250 ml/1 cup vegetable oil
4 tortillas (see page 26)
300 g/2 cups shredded,
   cooked chicken breast
shredded cabbage or iceberg
   lettuce
240 g/1 cup sour cream
90 g/1 cup grated/shredded
   cheese (your favourite type)

SERVES 2

Reheat the sauce in a pan over a low heat. Keep warm until needed.

Heat the oil in a frying pan/skillet over a medium-high heat. Take one tortilla and fry it for 10 seconds on each side. You must be able to fold the tortilla. If you fry the tortilla for too long, it will become very hard. If you don't fry it for long enough, it will tear easily.

Quickly dunk the fried tortilla into the warm sauce – this is a swift in-and-out dipping process. Immediately fold the dipped tortilla in half, fill it with shredded chicken and place on a serving plate. Repeat with the other tortillas – frying, dipping, folding and filling each one.

Drizzle any remaining sauce over the enchiladas, then finish them with the shredded cabbage or lettuce, sour cream and grated/shredded cheese.

BEAN ENFRIJOLADAS
ENFRIJOLADAS

This is the perfect way to use up leftover frijoles de la olla *from the day before.*

240 ml/1 cup vegetable oil
4 tortillas (see page 26)
240 g/1 cup sour cream

BEANS
150 ml/⅔ cup olive oil
1 quantity of Pot Beans
   (see page 32)

TO SERVE
shredded cabbage or iceberg
   lettuce
90 g/1 cup grated/shredded
   cheese (your favourite type)
120 g/1 cup pickled jalapeños

SERVES 2

Heat the olive oil in a saucepan over a medium heat. Add the beans and bring to the boil.

Heat the oil in a frying pan/skillet over a medium-high heat. Take one tortilla and fry it for 10 seconds on each side. You must be able to fold the tortilla. If you fry the tortilla for too long, it will become very hard. If you don't fry it for long enough, it will tear easily.

Quickly dunk the fried tortilla into the warm beans – this is a swift in-and-out dipping process. Immediately fold the dipped tortilla in half and place it on a serving plate. Repeat with the other tortillas – frying, dipping and folding each one.

Drizzle any remaining beans over the enchiladas, then finish with the cabbage or lettuce, sour cream, cheese and pickled jalapeños.

VARIATION *I sometimes add a fried or poached egg and some avocado slices on the side.*

MEXICAN-STYLE EGGS
HUEVOS A LA MEXICANA

I love this recipe. It is very simple, so is perfect when you are in a hurry but still want something tasty to eat. It makes a nice start to the day.

2 tablespoons vegetable oil
¼ white onion, finely chopped
200 g/7 oz. tomatoes, seeds
   removed and flesh cubed
4 eggs
10 g/¼ cup finely chopped
   fresh coriander/cilantro
salt and black pepper

TO SERVE
warm tortillas (see page 26)
Pot Beans (see page 32), warmed
grated/shredded cheese
   (your favourite type)

SERVES 2

Heat the oil in a saucepan over a medium heat. Add the onion and cook for about 5 minutes or until translucent. Add the tomatoes and a pinch of salt and cook for about 2 minutes or until softened.

Meanwhile, crack the eggs into a bowl, add some salt and pepper and beat vigorously with a fork. Add the beaten eggs to the pan and cook, stirring continuously to keep moving the eggs, until they are cooked to your liking. Add the coriander at the end and mix through.

Serve the scrambled eggs immediately with warm tortillas, the warmed beans and a handful of cheese.

SCRAMBLED EGGS WITH CHORIZO
HUEVOS CON CHORIZO

Definitely not the lightest breakfast but a very tasty one. I recommend serving with grated cheese and a sliced baguette.

½ tablespoon vegetable oil
¼ white onion, finely chopped
200 g/7 oz. spicy chorizo
4 eggs
20 g/¼ cup finely chopped
   fresh parsley
salt and black pepper

TO SERVE
warm tortillas (see page 26)
Pot Beans (see page 32),
   warmed, or sliced baguette
grated/shredded cheese
   (your favourite type)

SERVES 2

Heat the oil in a saucepan over a medium heat. Add the onion and cook for about 5 minutes or until translucent. Add the chorizo and a pinch of salt and cook for about 8–10 minutes or until the oil has been released from the chorizo and it is beginning to crisp.

Meanwhile, crack the eggs into a bowl, add some salt and pepper and beat vigorously with a fork. Add the beaten eggs to the pan and cook, stirring continuously to keep moving the eggs, until they are cooked to your liking. Add the parsley at the end and mix through.

Serve the scrambled eggs immediately with warm tortillas or sliced baguette, warmed beans and a handful of cheese.

Note In the UK the most similar spicy chorizo to Mexican types is the Spanish one; you can ask your local butcher also.

APPETIZERS

ENTRADAS

The dishes presented in this chapter are like a tour of the vast, multifaceted country that is Mexico. It is not only a geographical tour, but also an historical one. With almost 7,000 miles of coast, mountain ranges, deserts, tropical jungles, alpine forests, mangroves and river deltas, mine is one of the most biodiverse countries in the world.

Mexico is also home to many thriving native cultures, languages and cooking traditions and ways of relating to food. But despite this diversity, there exists a strong sense of cohesiveness. In every corner of the country, food is eaten with tortillas and salsas, but nowadays regional dishes like the Baja-style fish tacos (see page 52) or *sopecitos* (see page 68) from the central region are prepared all across Mexico. More importantly, no matter what they eat or what shape or colour their tortillas are, for every Mexican, food has a central and stellar place in their lives.

North of the Tropic of Cancer are the big deserts of Chihuahua and Sonora, but vast regions of these northern states are very fertile, crop yielding lands. The best Mexican wines come from the north of the country, either the Valley of Guadalupe in Baja California in the northwest (where some of the recipes in this chapter come from), or the Coahuila desert in the northeast. One of the key cultural differences between this region and the rest of Mexico is that they eat more wheat-flour tortillas (made with lard, wheat flour and water), the ones used for burritos.

The central high plateau (*altiplano*) is where most of the recipes come from in this chapter. Despite the name, this region is not flat at all. Mexico City is at the centre of it culturally and economically. And it is where I am from.

Volcanoes dominate the landscape across several states in the region geographers call the Trans-Mexican Volcanic Belt. Volcanoes supply the rich soil where the *milpas* grow (see page 10), along with a great variety of fruit trees like avocado, mango, guava, tamarind, many kinds of citrus, plums and, of course, flowering trees like *jacarandas*, *colorines* and *galeanas* (the dramatic African tulip tree). Among them, the magnificent *nopales* (known in English as prickly pears) and wild or cultivated agaves have been used since ancient times in Mexico for food, drink and medicine.

The south of Mexico is mostly Maya country. The descendants of this magnificent culture, around 5 million of them, still occupy this territory – from the highlands of Chiapas facing the Pacific Ocean to the flatlands of the Yucatán peninsula, inhabiting some of Mexico's most beautiful landscapes. As diverse as Europeans, Mayans speak different languages and have kept their ways of life and traditions, in some cases adapting them and keeping them secret. The *panuchos* (see page 71), the *sopa de lima* (see page 63) and the *salbutes* (see page 72) in this chapter are all from the Yucatán peninsula, but they can be eaten all over Mexico, specially the delicious and almost medicinal *sopa de lima*.

The southern states of Tabasco and Veracruz on the Gulf of Mexico could be considered a cultural region on its own. In this same coast, the Totonac people were the first to cultivate the vanilla orchid around the 10th century – and accidentally, they were the ones who welcomed Hernán Cortés when he disembarked in what later would become the city and port of Veracruz.

To finish this very general overview, I must mention the state of Oaxaca in the southwest, with its rough, mountainous landscape where pre-Hispanic traditions and languages have been pristinely preserved. I visited this state on my last trip to Mexico and had the chance to work with a traditional cook, Juana Amaya Hernandez and learn cooking techniques and recipes from her. Thanks to people like her, who have inherited the techniques and knowledge of generations, we can still enjoy truly authentic Mexican cooking.

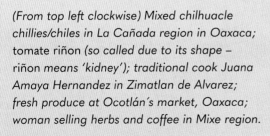

(From top left clockwise) Mixed chilhuacle chillies/chiles in La Cañada region in Oaxaca; tomate riñon (so called due to its shape – riñon means 'kidney'); traditional cook Juana Amaya Hernandez in Zimatlan de Alvarez; fresh produce at Ocotlán's market, Oaxaca; woman selling herbs and coffee in Mixe region.

BAJA-STYLE FISH TACOS
TACOS ESTILO BAJA CALIFORNIA

*This recipe is inspired by the traditional street tacos in Baja California.
Here, this variation uses a gluten-free tempura or batter.*

1 litre/4 cups rapeseed oil,
    for deep-frying
10 pieces of fish, each weighing
    about 80 g/3 oz. and 10–12 cm/
    4–5 in. long
10 tortillas, at least 12 cm/
    5 in. diameter (see page 26)
120 g/2 cups of shredded cabbage,
    white, red or a mixture of both
salt and ground white pepper

TEMPURA/BATTER
400 g/3 cups dried nixtamalized
    corn flour
50 g/3½ tablespoons Dijon
    mustard
1 teaspoon freshly ground
    black pepper
1 tablespoon table salt
1 litre/4 cups sparkling water

TO SERVE
3 limes, sliced
Avocado Salsa (see page 22)
any of your favourite salsas and
    sauces (see pages 19–25)
micro herbs or salad leaves,
    to garnish (optional)

MAKES 10 TACOS

First, make the batter. Place the corn flour, mustard, pepper, salt and half the sparkling water in a food processor and blend together. Add the rest of the sparkling water and blend again to a smooth batter. It should be thick enough to coat the fish, rather than slide straight off. If the batter seems too thick, add more water. Set aside until needed.

Heat the oil in a deep heavy-based saucepan to 170°C/325°F on a cooking thermometer.

Season the fish all over with salt and white pepper. Working in batches, dip each piece of fish into the batter so that it is completely coated, then carefully lower them in the hot oil. Cook for 2 minutes or until the batter has turned golden all over. Repeat until all of the fish pieces have been deep-fried.

Warm the tortillas in a large dry pan over a high heat for 1 minute on each side.

Add the shredded cabbage to the tortillas and top with the fried fish. Serve the fish tacos with the lime slices, avocado salsa, any of your favourite sauces and a handful of micro herbs or salad leaves.

Note As this is a gluten-free batter, the consistency will be slightly thicker than a normal batter.

SINALOA-STYLE AGUACHILE

AGUACHILE ESTILO SINALOA

Sinaloa is very well known for this dish. It's so simple but so good as an appetizer. I definitely recommend enjoying it with a cold beer. The prawns/ shrimps really need to be very fresh – I suggest going to your local fishmonger to ask for the largest and freshest prawns available.

20 raw prawns/shrimps, cleaned, shelled, deveined and cut in half
350 ml/1½ cups freshly squeezed lime juice
2 tablespoons sea salt
1–2 fresh green chillies/chiles, finely chopped (depending on how spicy you like your food)
1 red onion, thinly sliced
1 cucumber, halved lengthways and thinly sliced

TO SERVE
tostadas (see page 29)
avocado salsa (see page 22)

SERVES 4

Place all the ingredients in a large bowl and stir gently to mix everything together. Taste and adjust the seasoning if needed. Leave to rest for 1 minute. After 1 minute, serve the aguachile straight away with the tostadas and avocado salsa.

Note Always use the freshest prawns you can find from a trusted fishmonger or supplier.

MOOLI & POMEGRANATE CEVICHE

CEVICHE DE DAIKON Y GRANADA

A unique ceviche inspired by the Yucatán peninsula, this is a simple recipe, yet it has an amazingly deep flavour.

1 sharon fruit/persimmon, peeled and cut into cubes
1 mooli, peeled and cut in cubes
200 g/7 oz. pomegranate seeds
½ avocado, stoned/pitted, peeled and cut into cubes
1 tablespoon good-quality olive oil
sea salt

SAUCE
½ habanero chilli/chile, seeds removed, asado (see Note opposite)
1 onion, asado
juice of 2–3 limes
2 teaspoons good-quality olive oil
1 teaspoon sea salt

TO SERVE
lemon balm leaves or micro mizuna
olive oil, for drizzling
tostadas (see page 29) or tortilla chips

SERVES 2

To make the sauce, blend the charred habanero chilli and onion in a food processor with the lime juice, olive oil and salt. Add a bit of water to loosen the sauce if needed. It should be a runny sauce, rather than super thick.

Mix the sharon fruit, mooli, pomegranate seeds and avocado together in a bowl and season with a pinch of sea salt. Add the olive oil and the sauce and gently stir together. Divide the ceviche between serving plates or bowls. Finish with the lemon balm leaves or micro mizuna and drops of olive oil. Serve with tostadas or tortilla chips.

Note Asado or asada means that a vegetable has been cooked over hot coals or in a hot pan over a high heat until charred all over. See page 188 for a full explanation.

CAESAR SALAD
ENSALADA CESAR

It is believed that the Caesar salad originated from Cesar's Restaurant in Baja California Norte and was created by Caesar Cardini, an Italian immigrant. At the restaurant, the Caesar dressing is prepared fresh in front of the guests in an extra-large wooden bowl. It is definitely one of the best places to try it.

1 large Romaine/cos lettuce, leaves separated and cleaned
180 g/½ cup croutons
1 tablespoon finely grated/ shredded Grana Padano cheese

CAESAR DRESSING
1 egg yolk
1 garlic clove
¾ tablespoon Dijon mustard
3 tablespoons finely grated/ shredded Grana Padano cheese or Parmesan
juice of 1 large lime
1 tablespoon Worcestershire sauce
6–8 good-quality anchovies in oil
pinch of freshly ground black pepper
120 ml/½ cup vegetable or olive oil (not too strong a flavour)

SERVES 2–3

First, make the dressing. Place the egg yolk, garlic, mustard, cheese, lime juice, Worcestershire sauce, anchovies and black pepper in a mixing bowl. Use a handheld stick/immersion blender to blitz everything together to a paste. Slowly add the oil and whisk until the dressing has emulsified and all come together into a creamy consistency. Taste and adjust the seasoning if needed.

Place the lettuce leaves in a large mixing bowl. Drizzle over the dressing and toss until all the leaves are well coated in the dressing. Tip the leaves onto a serving platter, top with the croutons and sprinkle with the cheese before serving.

TARASCA SOUP

SOPA TARASCA

This is a soup from the Michoacan region. It is the perfect dish to warm you up on a really cold day.

2 ancho chillies/chiles – 1 left whole and 1 cut into very thin strips

3 tomatoes, asados (see Note below), then chopped

½ small white onion, asado

1 garlic clove, asada

1 litre/4 cups chicken stock

120 ml/½ cup olive oil, plus extra for frying

400 g/2 cups cooked bayos beans (or your favourite type of bean)

1 fresh bay leaf

½ tablespoon freshly ground black pepper

sea salt

TO SERVE

sour cream

fresh cheese (such as feta), cut into cubes

1 avocado, stoned/pitted, peeled and cut into cubes

8 tortillas (see page 26), cut into very thin strips and deep-fried

SERVES 6–8

Heat a dry frying pan/skillet or comal (see page 188) over a high heat and quickly toast the whole ancho chilli for about 5 seconds on each side, then remove.

Put the charred whole chilli in a food processor with the blackened tomatoes, onion and garlic and blend until smooth. Add a little chicken stock to loosen the mixture, if needed. Strain through a fine-mesh sieve/strainer.

Heat the olive oil in a saucepan over a medium heat. Add the sieved tomatoes and cook for 5 minutes.

Meanwhile, blend the beans with the chicken stock in a food processor, then strain and add to the pan with the tomatoes. Season with salt and pepper and add the bay leaf. Cook for 15 minutes, adding more stock if needed, until the soup is creamy.

Heat a little oil in a frying pan/skillet and quickly fry the sliced ancho chilli for 5 seconds. If fried for any longer, the chilli will became bitter.

Ladle the soup into bowls and swirl in some sour cream. Place a few cubes of cheese and avocado on top of the soup. Finish each bowl of soup with a handful of the deep-fried tortilla strips and the fried ancho chilli strips.

Note Asado or asada means that a vegetable has been cooked over hot coals or in a hot pan over a high heat until charred all over, see page 188 for a full explanation.

BERGAMOT SOUP

SOPA DE LIMA

This recipe from Yucatán is a regional delicacy and is definitely my favourite soup. In Mexico, lima is a type of sweet lemon called bergamot.

60 ml/¼ cup vegetable oil
1 white onion, thinly sliced
1 garlic clove, finely chopped
2 tomatoes, blanched in hot water
    for 1 minute, then skins and
    seeds removed and flesh cut
    into cubes
1 teaspoon ground cinnamon
pinch of ground cumin
pinch of freshly ground black
    pepper
1 habanero chilli/chile, thinly sliced
    (seeds and veins removed if you
    don't want too much heat)
4 bergamot (or limes), seeds
    removed and sliced
2 tortillas (see page 26), cut into
    very thin strips and deep-fried

POACHED CHICKEN
1 skinless and boneless chicken
    breast
2 garlic cloves
2 cloves
salt

SERVES 4

First, prepare the chicken. Put the chicken, garlic, cloves, 2 pinches of salt and 480 ml/2 cups water in a saucepan and bring to the boil. Continue to cook on a medium heat for 20–25 minutes until the chicken is cooked through. Strain the chicken broth into a jug/pitcher and set aside for later. Shred the chicken meat.

Heat the oil in a saucepan over a medium heat. Add the onions and cook for 5 minutes or until they are translucent. Add the garlic and cook for 1 minute, then add the tomatoes, the rest of the spices and the habanero chilli and cook for about 10 minutes until the tomatoes have started to break down. Add the reserved chicken stock and bring to the boil. Add the sliced bergamot or limes, turn off the heat and leave it to infuse for a couple of minutes.

Ladle the soup into serving bowls. Place some of the shredded chicken on top of the soup. Finish each bowl of soup with a handful of the fried tortilla strips and another slice or squeeze of bergamot or lime if liked.

Note This soup can also be served with some cubes of avocado or thin strips of mixed bell peppers on top if liked.

MUSHROOM SOUP

SOPA DE HONGOS

This soup is very common in the state of Mexico. The region is surrounded by forests and the weather is generally colder, which makes this soup very popular.

200 ml/scant 1 cup vegetable oil
½ white onion, thinly sliced
3 garlic cloves, finely chopped
350 g/4 cups sliced mushrooms (use whatever types are in season)
400 g/2 cups chopped tomatoes
1 litre/4 cups vegetable or chicken stock
40 g/1 cup chopped fresh coriander/cilantro, plus extra to garnish
salt and freshly ground black pepper

SERVES 4

Heat the oil in a saucepan over a medium-high heat. Add the onion and cook for 5 minutes or until translucent. Add the garlic and cook for about 2 minutes. Add the mushrooms, season with salt and black pepper and cook for about 5 minutes. Add the tomatoes and cook for about 8 minutes, then add the stock. Leave it to boil for about 5 minutes, then add the coriander and stir through. Taste and adjust the seasoning if needed. Simmer for about 20 minutes, then serve garnished with a little extra chopped coriander if liked.

AZTEC SOUP
SOPA DE TORTILLA

A very popular recipe from the central region in Mexico.

1 dried guajillo and 1 dried pasilla chilli/chile, veins and seeds removed (or use 1½ tablespoons chipotle chillies/chiles in adobo paste from a jar or can)

150 ml/⅔ cup olive oil

2 garlic cloves, chopped

½ white onion, chopped

1.5 kg/3¼ lb. tomatoes, chopped

2 x 15-cm/6-in. tortillas (see page 26), deep-fried and cut into strips

1 litre/4 cups chicken or vegetable stock

2 fresh epazote sprigs or 1 teaspoon hoja santa powder

1½ tablespoons sea salt

TO SERVE
sour cream

200 g/7 oz. fresh cheese (such as feta or Polish *twarog*)

1 avocado, stoned/pitted, peeled and cut into cubes

8 tortillas (see page 26), cut into thin strips and deep-fried until crisp

1 pasilla chilli/chile, cut into thin strips and lightly toasted in a pan with 2 tablespoons oil

SERVES 6–8

Soak the dried chillies in a bowl of warm water for about 1 hour. Drain the chillies, reserving their soaking water if you want to use it to add more heat to the dish.

Heat the oil in a saucepan over a medium-high heat. Add the garlic and onion and cook for about 3 minutes. Once they begin to colour, add the tomatoes and soaked chillies (or chipotle chillies) and cook for about 10 minutes. Add half the deep-fried tortillas and the stock and cook for a further 5 minutes.

Add the epazote or hoja santa, then use a handheld stick/immersion blender to blend the soup until smooth. Strain through a fine-mesh sieve/strainer and return to the pan to heat through again. Taste and add more salt if needed. Add more stock if the soup is too thick.

Ladle the soup into bowls and swirl in some sour cream. Place a few cubes of cheese and avocado on top of the soup. Finish each bowl with a handful of the deep-fried tortilla strips and toasted chilli strips.

BEAN-TOPPED SOPECITOS
SOPECITOS

This is another popular street food that works very well as an appetizer. This is the basic version with refried beans, but you can also make it with chicken, minced/ground beef, pumpkin flowers or any other vegetable or meat.

500 g/1 lb. 2 oz. nixtamalized
    corn dough (see page 26)
1 tablespoon salt

REFRIED BEANS
2 tablespoons duck fat or
    1 tablespoon pork fat
    or vegetable oil
¼ white onion, finely chopped
1 large garlic clove, finely chopped
300 g/2 cups Pot Beans
    (see page 32)
½ tablespoon avocado leaf powder
    or 10 g/¼ cup chopped fresh
    coriander/cilantro
salt

TO SERVE
240 g/1 cup sour cream
75 g/2 cups shredded iceberg
    lettuce
½ red onion, finely chopped
100 g/1 cup fresh cheese (feta or
    similar), crumbled or grated/
    shredded
any of your favourite salsas and
    sauces (see pages 19–25)

SERVES 4

First, make the refried beans. Heat the fat or oil in a saucepan over a medium heat. Add the onion and cook for about 1 minute. Add the garlic and let it take on a bit of colour, then add the cooked beans and a pinch of salt. Keep mixing and smashing the beans for 4–5 minutes, until you are left with a beany mash. Season with the avocado leaf powder or chopped coriander. Add a cup of water if needed – the mixture should be moist and not too dry.

Preheat a large frying pan/skillet over a medium heat.

Take a ball of nixtamalized corn dough roughly the size of your fist, work it briefly in your hands, then shape it into a fat tortilla about 5–8 mm/¼–½ inches thick. Cook the tortilla on one side for about 1 minute, then flip and cook for about 2 minutes on the other side, before flipping again. Pinch the edges of the tortilla to make a sopecito with raised sides to contain the beans. Continue to cook the sopecito for a further 5–6 minutes, flipping it a couple more times to make sure the dough is cooked properly or until it is a bit crispy on the outside. Repeat until you have used up all the dough, making around 8–12 sopecitos depending on their size.

Place the sopecitos on a serving plate and fill each one with a spoonful of beans. Finish with some sour cream, lettuce, red onion, cheese and your preferred salsas and sauces.

PANUCHOS
PANUCHOS

Panuchos is one of the best-loved street foods in the Yucatán peninsula, and definitely one of my favourites. It requires a bit more precision when making the tortillas because the tortillas have to puff up for the panuchos, otherwise it is impossible to fill them with the refried beans.

400 g/14 oz. nixtamalized corn dough (see page 26)
220 g/1½ cups Refried Beans (see page 68, made with black beans), placed in a piping/pastry bag
240 ml/1 cup pork fat or duck fat or vegetable oil
500 g/1 lb. 2 oz. Pibil-style Pork (see page 129)
pickled red onions, to serve

SERVES 4

Take a ball of the nixtamalized corn dough that weighs about 25 g/1 oz. Use a tortilla press to make small tortillas (called taquera size). Heat a large, dry frying pan/skillet over a medium-high heat. One at a time, add the tortillas. As soon as they puff up, make a hole just large enough to insert the piping bag and fill each one with refried beans. Transfer the filled panuchos to a dish and keep covered with a damp, clean dish towel.

Heat the fat or oil in the same pan over a medium heat and fry the panuchos for about 1 minute, flipping them several times. Place the cooked panuchos on a large serving plate.

In a separate pan, warm up the pibil-style pork. Once hot, spoon some over each panuchos and finish with pickled red onions on top.

CHILEATOLE
CHILEATOLE

This recipe I learned in Tlaxacala or to be more exact in San Felipe Ixtacuixtla, which is my grandpa's home town. It is simple, but very tasty. I remember it being sold from street stalls, especially during harvest time.

1.5 litres/6 cups chicken or vegetable stock or water
460 g/3 cups fresh corn kernels (we use the white variety)
120 g/½ cup nixtamalized corn dough (see page 26)
1 tablespoon salt
4 tablespoons chopped fresh coriander/cilantro, plus extra to serve
2 jalapeños or green chillies/chiles (yellow chillies/chiles also work)

SERVES 6–8

Pour 1 litre/4 cups of the stock or water into a saucepan and add the fresh corn kernels. Bring to the boil and continue cooking for 15 minutes until they are soft and cooked through.

Blend the corn dough or fresh corn kernels with 240 ml/1 cup of the stock or water, then strain. Add this mixture to the pan with the cooked corn and continue to cook, stirring continuously to avoid it sticking to the pan. Season to taste.

Blend the coriander, chillies and the remaining stock or water in a food processor, then strain. Add this mixture to the pan. Taste and add more salt if needed. Serve the chileatole with some extra coriander leaves on top.

SALBUTES

SALBUTES

This dish is very common in the Yucatán peninsula. The size of the tortilla varies depending on the location, but it is basically semi-cooked tortilla usually between 20–30 cm/8–12 inches in diameter, that is deep-fried until puffy and crunchy. It is served stuffed with chicken, but you could also use pork, venison or turkey.

1 whole chicken
   (weighing about 1.8 kg/4 lb.)
a few drops of lime juice
1 white onion, cut in half, one half
   asada, one cut into half moons
1 whole garlic bulb, asada
1 fresh güero chilli/chile, asado
   (or any variety of yellow chilli)
1 tablespoon dried Mexican
   oregano
1 tablespoon salt
2 teaspoons black pepper
6 bay leaves
60 g/½ cup pickled jalapeños
1 litre/4 cups vegetable oil
500 g/1 lb. 2 oz. nixtamalized corn
   dough (see page 26)

ESCABECHE MIX
½ tablespoon ground cinnamon
½ teaspoon ground cloves
½ tablespoon ground cumin
1 tablespoon allspice powder
½ teaspoon garlic powder
6 bay leaves
2 tablespoons freshly ground
   black pepper

LIGHTLY PICKLED ONIONS
1 red onion, thinly sliced
1 tablespoon salt, plus extra pinch
juice of 2 oranges
1 teaspoon white wine vinegar

TO SERVE
120 g/2 cups shredded white
   cabbage
1 tomato, finely sliced
avocado slices
lime wedges, for squeezing

SERVES 6–8

First, prepare the escabeche mix. Combine all the ingredients in a small bowl, add 60 ml/¼ cup water and mix together.

Rinse the chicken with fresh water and a few drops of lime juice. Place the chicken in a large saucepan and add the escabeche mix, rubbing it all over the chicken so that. Leave for 5 minutes to marinate.

Add enough water to just cover the chicken and bring it to the boil. Skim off any foam that rises to the top. Add the charred onion, garlic and güero chilli and cook for about 10 minutes. Add the oregano, salt, black pepper, bay leaves and the sliced onion and cook for about 1 hour or until the juices run clear when you pierce the chicken in the thickest part. Once the chicken is cooked, add the pickled jalapeños, then turn off the heat. Leave it to cool down a little, then shred the chicken meat and set aside until needed.

Next, prepare the pickled onions. Mix the red onion with 1 tablespoon of the salt, leave for 5 minutes and then rinse. Mix the onion with the rest of the ingredients in a bowl and leave to pickle for about 10 minutes.

Preheat the oil in a large, heavy-based saucepan to 170°C/325°F.

Take a ball of the nixtamalized corn dough and shape it into a tortilla between 20–30 cm/8–12 inches in diameter. Lightly cook the tortilla in a large, dry frying pan/skillet, flipping it from one side to the other, for 30 seconds at a time. Lower this lightly cooked tortilla into the hot oil. It will start to puff up straight away. Cook for a few seconds until it has puffed up and is a little crunchy, then carefully remove the salbute to a bowl or plate lined with kitchen paper to absorb any excess oil. Repeat with the rest of the dough until you have about 6–8 puffed salbutes.

Place the chicken on top of the salbutes. Add the cabbage, tomato, avocado and serve with the pickled onions and lime wedges.

Note Asado or asada means that a vegetable has been cooked over hot coals or in a hot pan over a high heat until charred all over. See page 188 for a full explanation.

BLACK BEANS WITH CORN DOUGH DUMPLINGS

FRIJOLES CON CHOCHOYOTES

This recipe is very special to me. It is incredibly simple but the chochoyotes give it a lovely texture. I recommend using hoja santa and avocado leaf powders if you can get hold of them, as they make a big difference to the end result.

250 g/9 oz. nixtamalized corn dough (see page 26)
40 g/½ cup grated/shredded fresh cheese (such as feta)
radishes, thinly sliced, to serve
fresh coriander/cilantro leaves, to serve

BEANS
500 g/2 cups pinto beans, rinsed
½ white onion, cut in half
½ garlic bulb, just washed
½ tablespoon hoja santa powder
1 teaspoon avocado leaf powder
salt

SERVES 4

Put the beans into a saucepan along with the onion, garlic and 2 pinches of salt. Pour in enough water to cover the beans and cook over a low heat for about 1 hour, or until soft. Remove and discard the garlic and onion, then add the hoja santa and avocado leaf powders. Simmer for a further 20 minutes.

Meanwhile, mix the nixtamalized corn dough with the cheese and a pinch of salt in a bowl. The mixture should be easy to handle, but if you feel it is too hard, add a bit of water. Take a ball of the corn dough that weighs about 5–10 g/¼ oz. Make a small indentation in the middle of the ball. Repeat with the rest of the dough, then add the dough balls to the beans. Keep an eye on the beans as the dumplings can make the mixture quite thick. Add more water to keep the beans at a soupy consistency if needed.

PRAWN TOSTADAS
TOSTADAS DE CAMARON

Seafood is a very important part of Mexican cuisine, not only in the states with a coastline but also in major cities where you can find restaurants serving fresh seafood. I feel very connected to Mexican seafood and use it often in my cooking.

15 large raw prawns/shrimps, shelled and deveined
½ red onion, diced
75 g/½ cup diced cucumber, with seeds removed
20 g/½ cup chopped fresh coriander/cilantro
160 g/1 cup diced tomato, with seeds removed
120 ml/½ cup fresh lime juice
2 tablespoons olive oil
1 green Thai chilli/chile, finely chopped
sea salt

TO SERVE
8 tostadas (see page 29)
480 ml/2 cups Avocado Salsa (see page 22)
40 g/1 cup chopped fresh coriander/cilantro
any of your favourite salsas or sauces (see pages 19–25) (optional)

SERVES 2–3

Fill a saucepan with 1 litre/4 cups water, add a pinch of sea salt and bring to the boil.

Prepare a bowl of iced water.

Drop the prawns into the boiling water and cook them for about 25 seconds. Quickly transfer them to the iced water to give them a thermal shock. Immediately take them out of the iced water and drain as well as possible. Cut the prawns into cubes that are no larger than 1 cm/½ inch.

Put all of the remaining ingredients for the prawns in a bowl along with the cooked prawns and mix together. Taste and adjust the salt if needed.

Place the tostadas on a serving plate, spoon some of the avocado salsa over each one, then top with the prawn mixture and add more sauce if you wish. Garnish with the chopped coriander leaves and serve with your favourite spicy sauce if preferred.

MEMELITAS
MEMELITAS

This Oaxacan street food is very similar to the sopecitos *from the central area (see page 68), the difference is the amount of* asiento (pork fat) *that people use in this region.* Asiento *is the last part of the pork fat after frying the* chicharrón (pork rinds). *Another difference is the use of* quesillo (Queso Oaxaca), *which is similar to mozzarella.*

500 g/1 lb. 2 oz. nixtamalized
   corn dough (see page 26)
1 tablespoon salt
120 ml/½ cup water
240 ml/1 cup sour cream
115 g/1 cup grated/shredded
   cheese (*queso Oaxaca*,
   mozzarella or similar)
240 ml/1 cup Red or Green Sauce
   (see page 25)

REFRIED BEANS
2 tablespoons duck fat or
   1 tablespoon pork fat
   (or vegetable oil), plus extra
   for topping
2 tablespoons finely chopped
   white onion
1 large garlic clove, finely chopped
300 g/2 cups Pot Beans
   (see page 32)
½ tablespoon avocado leaf powder
   or 10 g/¼ cup chopped fresh
   coriander/cilantro

SERVES 4

First, make the refried beans. Heat the fat or oil in a saucepan over a medium heat. Add the onion and cook for about 1 minute. Add the garlic and let it take on a bit of colour, then add the cooked beans and a pinch of salt. Keep mixing and smashing the beans for 4–5 minutes, until you are left with a beany mash. Season with the avocado leaf powder or chopped coriander. Add a cup of water if needed – the mixture should be moist and not too dry.

Preheat a large, dry frying pan/skillet over a medium heat.

Take a ball of nixtamalized corn dough roughly the size of your fist (about 30 g/1 oz.), work it briefly in your hands, then shape it into a fat tortilla about 5–8 mm/¼–½ inches thick. Cook the tortillas on one side for about 1 minute, then flip and cook for about 2 minutes on the other side before flipping again. Pinch the edges of the tortillas to make a memelita with raised sides to contain the beans. Continue to cook the memelita for a further 5–6 minutes, flipping it to make sure the dough is cooked properly or until it is a bit crispy on the outside. Repeat until you have used up all the dough, making around 16 small memelitas.

Add a small amount of pork fat on top of each memelita, then a spoonful of beans, then top with some some cheese. Continue to cook for a further 2 minutes until the cheese has melted. Transfer to a serving plate and serve the memelitas with both green and red sauces if you wish.

Note In this region, people use pasilla Oaxaqueño, *a smoked chilli/ chile from the Mixe region, which is definitely my favourite dried chilli.*

NORTHERN-STYLE STUFFED PEPPERS

CHILES RELLENO NORTEÑO

This is one of the most representative dishes from the northern regions in Mexico. Poblano chillies/chiles are stuffed with minced/ground beef or pork, baked and served with a delicious sauce.

4 poblano chillies/chiles (or a similar variety – Anaheim or even bell peppers work)
180 g/2 cups grated/shredded cheese
20 g/½ cup chopped fresh parsley, to serve

FILLING
100 ml/scant ½ cup vegetable oil
1 onion, finely chopped
6 garlic cloves, finely chopped
1 potato, peeled and diced
1 carrots, peeled and diced
500 g/1 lb. 2 oz. minced/ground beef or pork
pinch of ground cumin
2 tablespoons salt
1 tablespoon ground black pepper
40 g/1 cup chopped fresh parsley

TOMATO SAUCE
8–9 tomatoes, quartered
¼ onion, cut into 3 pieces
1½ tablespoons salt
50 ml/3½ tablespoons vegetable oil

SERVES 4

First, make the filling. Heat the oil in a saucepan over a high heat. Add the onion and cook for about 1 minute, stirring continuously. Add the garlic, and after another minute, add the potatoes and carrots. Cook for about 3 minutes. Add the minced meat and cook while moving it constantly to break up the meat and ensure that it cooks evenly. Lower the heat to avoid burning the meat, then add the cumin, salt, pepper and parsley and cook for a further 15 minutes until the meat has browned. Continue to cook until the meat juices have reduced by half. Set aside until needed.

Char the chillies over a direct flame or with a blowtorch until the skins have blackened all over. When the chillies are cool enough to handle, remove the skins. Make a slit in each chilli lengthways, just long enough to be able to stuff them. Carefully clean the insides, keeping the shape of the chillies as far as possible. Stuff the chillies with the filling mixture and seal them closed with a toothpick. Place the stuffed chillies on a baking sheet lined with non-stick parchment paper.

To make the sauce, blend the tomatoes, onion and salt together in a food processor or blender and then strain through a fine-mesh sieve/strainer. Heat the oil in a saucepan over a high heat, then add the tomato mixture. Let it boil for about 5 minutes, then add 500 ml/2 cups water and bring back to the boil. Taste and add more salt if needed. Keep simmering on a low heat.

Preheat the oven to 180°C/160°C fan/350°F/Gas 4. Sprinkle the stuffed chillies with the cheese and place in the oven for 15 minutes, or until the chillies have warmed through and the cheese has melted.

Spoon the warm tomato sauce into a deep serving plate and nestle the stuffed chillies in the sauce. Scatter over the chopped parsley before serving.

STREET FOOD
ANTOJITOS

Most of Mexico is blessed with a wonderful climate all year round. Of course, there are differences between the regions of the country, but in general there are two main seasons in the year: the dry one, from October to March, and the rainy one, from April to September. The dry season coincides with the winter and the spring, and the rainy season with the summer and the autumn/fall. Despite the climatic differences, some people like to say we have an eternal spring in Mexico, and they may well be right.

This fine weather naturally brings people out onto the streets, and consequently, street food is everywhere. Queueing at a street food stall fosters casual conversations with strangers more than in any restaurant. Across every town and city, you will find all kinds of street food vendors at all times of the day and night. From morning until midnight, the streets have their own rhythm marked by food.

The morning is for the juice stalls, well equipped with cold-press juicers and smoothie blenders. They also offer creative fruit, vegetable and cereal combos to start the day. On street corners, in parks and outside larger subway stations, freshly cut fruit seasoned with lemon, salt and chilli/chile powder is sold from beautiful carts fitted with glass boxes. The way the sellers cut these fruits is a pure art form. Mexican street food vendors are very resourceful. The 'stall' might only be a basket in which mangoes cut in fancy ways are displayed, or a supermarket trolley full of oranges with a board balanced on top to rest the type of cast-iron juicer that I have not seen outside of Mexico.

Tamales are sold at any time of the day in Mexico, as they can be eaten for breakfast, lunch or dinner. Depending on where you are, you will find *tamales* in different shapes or wrapped in different ways (much like the way bread comes in all sorts of shapes in Europe). *Corundas* (see page 86) are a *tamal* from Michoacán that has a conical, or even pyramidal, shape. Some tamales are wrapped in banana leaves and called *oaxaqueños*, others in corn husks. The tamales sellers are constantly in motion, normally on their bikes fitted with large baskets or a cylindrical steamer to keep the food warm. The sound of their voice announcing their presence can always be heard in the background in any Mexican city: 'Warm tamales, delicious tamales!'

All day long, you will also find vendors, usually women, with big round *comales* (cast-iron pans) set over portable gas burners to cook *quesadillas*, *tlacoyos* and, if you are in Oaxaca, *tlayudas*. I love the clever way these women build a complete and often very clean kitchen on a street corner: with an umbrella or a plastic awning for shade, a few plastic stools, the *comal* and the gas burner, a big bucket with their masa dough to make fresh tortillas, and all their *guisados* (the already cooked and prepared fillings for quesadillas) neatly stored in containers. They often use thin plastic bags to cover the plates so there is no need to wash anything, and offer two or three salsas to go with your food.

In parks where children play, you will find plenty of salty, crunchy and sweet foodstuffs. There are crispy potato chips and – everyone's favourite – boiled corn on the cob/ears of corn smeared in mayonnaise and sprinkled with cheese and chilli/chile powder. Occasionally the corn cobs will be grilled over hot coals instead of boiled. Then there is *raspados* – shaved ice served in a cup and flavoured with colourful syrups with fancy names like 'raspberry unicorn' or 'jumpy bird'.

Living in Mexico you develop a sixth sense for cleanliness when it comes to street food vendors. Every Mexican has the voice of a food safety agent in their head to guide them, and if you follow your instincts, only very occasionally will one get sick with the infamous 'Moctezuma's revenge'. There's no chance of anyone getting sick with 'street food' made at home though. The recipes that follow are all inspired by common street foods in Mexico, and they are great to share with friends and family.

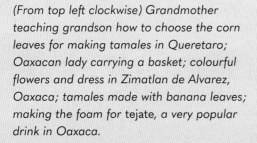

(From top left clockwise) Grandmother teaching grandson how to choose the corn leaves for making tamales in Queretaro; Oaxacan lady carrying a basket; colourful flowers and dress in Zimatlan de Alvarez, Oaxaca; tamales made with banana leaves; making the foam for tejate, a very popular drink in Oaxaca.

CORUNDAS
CORUNDAS

This is a type of tamal *from the Michoacán region. The most difficult ingredient to find is the corn leaves, which are the green leaves from the actual plant, not the husks from the ears of corn. If you can't find them, substitute banana leaves cut to 8–10 cm/3–4 inches wide and left as long as possible.*

18–20 green leaves from the corn plant, plus extra for lining the steamer
sour cream, to serve

DOUGH
300 g/10½ oz. duck fat or similar
2 tablespoons salt
1 kg/2¼ lb. nixtamalized corn dough (see page 26)
240 ml/1 cup water or chicken stock
1 tablespoon baking powder
1 small green (bell) pepper, seeds removed and finely chopped
1 large yellow chilli/chile, seeds and veins removed and finely chopped
½ white onion, finely chopped
1 small poblano pepper, seeds removed and finely chopped
115 g/1 cup finely grated/shredded soft fresh cheese (mozzarella or Polish *twarog* work well)

SALSA
1 tablespoon duck fat or vegetable oil
¼ white onion, finely chopped
2 garlic cloves, finely chopped
3 jalapeño chillies/chiles
4 tomatoes, asados (see Note below), skins and seeds removed
salt

MAKES 18–20

First, prepare the dough. Place the fat and salt in the bowl of an electric mixer fitted with the flat beater. Keep mixing until the fat is very soft and has become fluffy. Add the nixtamalized corn dough and mix for about 10 minutes. Slowly add the water or chicken stock and mix for 5 minutes. Add the baking powder and mix for a further 1 minute.

Transfer the dough to a mixing bowl and add all the chopped vegetables and the cheese to the dough. Incorporate everything by hand otherwise the vegetables will be chopped too fine.

Preheat a steamer.

Meanwhile, prepare the corundas. Take one corn leaf and place about 2 tablespoons of the dough right at the tip of the leaf. Start to close the leaf as though you are making a triangle shape. Make sure the last part of the leaf is tucked in tight to keep the dough in place. Repeat with all the leaves and dough.

Place some extra corn leaves in the base of the steamer and put the prepared corundas on top, followed by another layer of corn leaves. Leave to steam for about 1 hour.

Meanwhile, make the salsa. Heat the fat or oil in a saucepan over a medium heat. Add the onion and cook for 5 minutes or until translucent, then add the garlic. Once they have started to take on some colour, add the chillies and sauté for about 2 minutes. Transfer to a blender with the tomatoes and a pinch of salt and blend everything together to a very smooth sauce.

Arrange the corundas on a serving plate with bowls of the sour cream and salsa to drizzle over once the corundas are unwrapped.

Note Asado or asada means that a vegetable has been cooked over hot coals or in a hot pan over a high heat until charred all over. See page 188 for a full explanation.

CHALUPITAS

CHALUPITAS

Another street food that also works very well as an appetizer, this recipe is for the basic chalupita that is common in Tlaxcala state. There are many different ways to make them, with some 'pinching' the sides to create a type of little boat or just making the tortillas slightly thicker; it is up to you which method you choose. You can also serve the chalupitas with shredded chicken, pork or beef on top.

400 g/14 oz. nixtamalized
  corn dough (see page 26)
480 ml/2 cups vegetable oil
720 ml/3 cups Red Sauce
  (see page 25)
salt

TO SERVE
115 g/1 cup grated/shredded
  or crumbled fresh cheese
  (such as feta or similar)
½ red onion, finely chopped
240 ml/1 cup sour cream
Green Sauce (see page 25)
lime wedges, for squeezing over

SERVES 4

Preheat a large, dry frying pan/skillet over a medium heat.

Taste the nixtamalized corn dough and mix in a little salt and water if the dough needs a bit more moisture.

Take a ball of the dough weighing about 25 g/1 oz. (see Note below). Work it briefly in your hands, then shape it into a small tortilla. Cook the tortilla on one side for about 20 seconds, then flip and cook for another 1 minute on the other side, then flip again. Repeat until you have used up all the dough, making around 20 chalupitas.

Once all the chalupitas are cooked, add 3 tablespoons of the vegetable oil to the same pan over a medium heat. You could use pork fat instead if liked. Place a few of the chalupitas in the hot oil and fry for a few minutes until crisp, adding more oil as needed. Cover the chalupitas with some red sauce and continue frying for a further 1 minute. Repeat with the rest of the chalupitas and sauce, working in batches until all have been cooked.

Arrange the chalupitas on a serving plate or board. Finish with the grated/shredded cheese and scatter some red onion on top. Serve immediately with the sour cream and green sauce on the side.

ITACATES

ITACATES

This popular street food is most commonly found on street food stalls in the central region of Mexico.

500 g/1 lb. 2 oz. nixtamalized corn dough (see page 26)
1 tablespoon salt
230 g/1 cup goat curd (or any cheese that melts)
200 g/1 cup mashed potato

TO SERVE
240 ml/1 cup sour cream
60 g/2 cups finely chopped iceberg lettuce
115 g/1 cup grated/shredded or crumbled fresh cheese (such as feta or similar)
½ red onion, finely chopped
your favourite salsas or sauces (see pages 19–25)

tortilla press
2 thin sheets of plastic

SERVES 4

Taste the nixtamalized corn dough and mix in the salt and water if the dough needs a bit more moisture.

Take a ball of the corn dough weighing about 60 g/2 oz. Work it briefly in your hands, then roll it into a ball. Place it in a tortilla press and make a fat tortilla. Add a spoonful of the oat curd and a spoonful of the mashed potato in the centre, then fold the tortilla to form a triangle, making sure the filling is completely enclosed. Repeat until you have used up all the dough.

Preheat a large frying pan/skillet over a medium heat. Cook the itacates on one side for 2 minutes, then flip and cook on the other side for 2 minutes. Keep flipping to avoid burning the itacates. Once the dough is cooked through, golden and crisp, serve them with sour cream, lettuce, cheese, onion and your favourite salsas and sauces.

PUMPKIN FLOWER QUESADILLAS

QUESADILLAS DE FLOR DE CALABAZA

This is one of my favourite quesadillas. Unfortunately, it is impossible to find fresh epazote in the UK, but you can substitute this amazing herb with coriander/cilantro or parsley – not quite the same, but still tasty. Pumpkin flowers are very popular in Mexican markets, which means that the prices are really good for the amount of flowers they give you. In Europe, on the other hand, they are not as popular so the price can be quite high. They are still worth seeking out and if you grow your own pumpkins you should have a plentiful supply.

150 ml/⅔ cup vegetable oil
1 white onion, finely chopped
1 garlic clove, finely chopped
1 jalapeño chilli/chile, seeds removed and finely chopped
20 fresh pumpkin flowers, stems and pistils removed
20 g/½ cup chopped fresh coriander/cilantro or 10 g/¼ cup chopped fresh parsley
4 tortillas (see page 26)
250 g/3 cups grated/shredded cheese (mozzarella works well, or one that easily melts and is not too strong)
salt

SERVES 2

Heat the vegetable oil in a frying pan/skillet over a high heat. Add the onion and cook for 1 minute. Add the garlic and cook for another minute. Add the jalapeño chilli and the pumpkin flowers and season with some salt. Cook, stirring continuously to keep everything moving, then lower the heat to medium. Cook for about 10 minutes, then add the coriander or parsley. Taste and add more salt if needed. Transfer to a bowl and keep covered while you prepare the tortillas.

Heat a large, dry frying pan/skillet over a medium-high heat. Warm a tortilla, then add 1–2 spoonfuls of the pumpkin flower mixture and 1 tablespoon of the cheese all over one half of the tortilla. Fold the tortilla in half and cook on both sides until the cheese has melted. Repeat until you have used up all of the tortillas and pumpkin flower mixture. Serve immediately.

VARIATION: *Huitlacoche Quesadillas*
Huitlacoche is a corn fungus that has been used in Mexican cooking for hundreds of years. It is quite easy to get in Mexico, but not so easy to source elsewhere. Prepare the filling mixture as directed above but replace the pumpkin flowers with 200 g/7 oz. huitlacoche. Continue to make the quesadillas following the instructions above. Substitute with any other mushroom if you cannot get hold of huitlacoche.

BEAN & AVOCADO LEAF TLACOYOS

TLACOYOS DE FRIJOL CON HOJA DE AGUACATE

*This recipe is from the state of Tlaxcala in the central region of Mexico.
My grandma used to prepare these at her food stall in Mexico city
so it is a recipe very close to my heart.*

60 ml/¼ cup olive oil, plus extra
   for frying
¼ onion, finely chopped
2 garlic cloves, finely chopped
1½ teaspoons avocado leaf powder
500 g/1 lb. 2 oz. nixtamalized corn
   dough (see page 26)

BEANS
420 g/2 cups pinto beans, rinsed
½ white onion, cut in half
½ garlic bulb, washed and cut
   in half
sea salt

TO SERVE
90 g/1 cup grated/shredded or
   crumbled fresh cheese (such as
   feta or similar – I also use Grana
   Padano)
½ red onion, finely chopped
fresh coriander/cilantro leaves
any of your favourite salsas and
   sauces (I recommend Avocado
   Salsa, page 22, and Red Sauce,
   page 25)
240 g/1 cup sour cream

SERVES 2

First, prepare the beans. Place the beans in a saucepan of water with the onion, garlic and 2 pinches of salt and cook for about 1½ hours or until they are cooked. Once they are soft, remove and discard the garlic and onion and strain the beans, reserving the cooking water in case you need to rehydrateany leftover beans at a later stage (see Note below).

Heat the olive oil in a saucepan over a medium heat. Once hot, add the onion and cook for 5 minutes until it starts to take on a bit of colour, then add the garlic. Once the garlic takes on some colour, add the cooked beans, avocado leaf powder and a pinch of salt. Use a spoon to mash the beans until you have a rough purée – it should be similar in texture to the corn dough, quite thick but not stick to your hands that easily.

Take balls of the nixtamalized corn dough weighing about 60 g/2 oz. Shape each ball into a thick tortilla. Add a spoonful of the bean mixture to the centre of each tortilla. Wrap the tortilla around the bean mixture, making sure all the filling is fully enclosed in a smooth ball of dough. Start to form the dough into a flat diamond shape about 5 mm–1 cm/⅛–½ inches thick.

Heat a few drops of oil in a large frying pan/skillet over a medium heat. Add the tlacoyos and cook for 1 minute on each side, flipping them 4 times from one side to the other. Once they start to take on some colour, they are ready.

Arrange the tlacoyos on a large serving plate, add some cheese, onion and coriander leaves on top of each one. Serve the salsas and sauces and sour cream on the side, in a small bowls with a little spoon so everyone can add as much as they wish.

Note If you do not use all the beans for this recipe, you can keep them to serve for breakfast. Add a little of the reserved bean cooking water to loosen them a bit, then taste and adjust the seasoning before serving.

BEETROOT TLAYUDAS
TLAYUDAS DE BETABEL

*Tlayudas are very popular in Oaxaca. They are normally about
30–35 cm/12–14 inches long, but I have made them smaller here.*

TLAYUDA DOUGH
320 g/11 oz. nixtamalized
  corn dough (see page 26)
½ teaspoon sea salt

MORITA SAUCE
500 g/1 lb 2 oz. ripe tomatoes
4 morita chillies/chiles, seeds
  removed and soaked in warm
  water for a milder flavour
3 garlic cloves
½ white onion
sea salt

OAXACA-STYLE BEANS
500 g/2 cups pinto beans, rinsed
  and soaked in water overnight
1 white onion, cut in half
½ garlic bulb
1½ teaspoons hoja santa powder
1½ teaspoons avocado leaf powder
120 ml/½ cup olive oil

BEETROOT/BEETS
1 kg/2¼ lb. beetroot/beets, peeled
  and cut into 3-cm/1½-in. cubes
pinch of sea salt
pinch of freshly ground black
  pepper
pinch of Mexican dried oregano
2 tablespoons olive oil

TO SERVE
1 quantity of Avocado Purée
  (see Note on page 133)
1 baby candy beetroot/beet,
  thinly sliced (use a mandoline)
100 g/1 cup shoots or micro
  rocket/arugula

large tortilla press
2 thin sheets of plastic

SERVES 4

To make the tlayuda dough, mix the nixtamalized corn dough and salt together in a bowl for about 5 minutes, adding a bit of water if needed. The texture should be like modelling clay and stick easily to your hands. Take a ball of dough that weighs about 40 g/1½ oz. Use a tortilla press to make a thin tortilla – the tortilla should be as thin as possible, the thinner the better. Repeat until the rest of the dough has been used up.

Carefully place the tortilla in a large, dry pan over a high heat and cook for 1 minute on one side. Flip it over and cook for another minute. Flip it over again and keep turning until the tortilla is dry and crispy. Preheat the grill/broiler to high and finish the tlayudas under the hot grill until very crispy.

To make the morita sauce, place all the ingredients in a saucepan with 240 ml/1 cup water over a medium heat and bring to the boil. Continue cooking for about 10 minutes or until the tomatoes have broken down. Transfer everything to a food processor and blend until smooth. Taste and add more salt if needed. Pass through a fine-mesh sieve/strainer for an even smoother sauce.

Place the soaked beans in a saucepan with the onion, garlic and some salt and cover with water. Cook for 1–2 hours or until they are cooked and soft. Remove and discard the onion and garlic, then transfer the cooked beans to a food processor and blend with the hoja santa and avocado powders until smooth. Pass through a fine-mesh sieve/strainer to make an even smoother. Heat the oil in a saucepan over a medium heat. Add the blended beans and cook for about 15 minutes. Taste and adjust the seasoning if needed.

Preheat the oven to 120°C/100°C fan/250°F/Gas ½. Place the cubed beetroot on a baking sheet and cook in the preheated oven for about 2 hours or until cooked through. Sprinkle over the salt, black pepper and oregano, then drizzle with the oil.

Arrange the tlayudas on a serving plate and cover the surface of each one with the blended beans, followed by the avocado purée and top with the roasted beetroot. Drizzle over some morita sauce and finish with the sliced candy beetroot, pea shoots or micro rocket. Enjoy!

GRILLED BEEF TLAYUDAS
TLAYUDAS DE CARNE ASADA

This is the probably one of my favourite versions of the tlayuda and is very popular in Oaxaca. I recommend you cook them on a hot grill or barbecue as the smoky flavour really makes a difference to the finished dish.

1 quantity of Tlayuda Dough
(see page 97)
1 quantity of Oaxaca-style Beans
(see page 97)
2 tablespoons olive oil
sea salt

GRILLED BEEF
500 g/1 lb. 2 oz. beef steak
(use your favourite cut –
I prefer rib-eye or bavette)
2 pinches of sea salt
2 pinches of freshly ground
black pepper
pinch of Mexican dried oregano

TO SERVE
30 g/1 cup rocket/arugula
any of your favourite salsas and
sauces (see pages 19–25)

large tortilla press
2 thin sheets of plastic

SERVES 4

Make the tlayuda dough and cook the tlayudas following the instructions on page 97.

Make the Oaxaca-style beans following the instructions on page 97.

Season the beef with the salt, pepper and oregano. Preheat the grill/broiler or prepare a barbecue and wait until the coals are hot. Cook the steak to your liking – I normally cook it for about 4 minutes on each side for medium rare, then rest the meat before slicing.

Heat the oil in a saucepan over a medium heat. Add the beans and cook for about 15 minutes. Taste and adjust the seasoning if needed.

Arrange the tlayudas on a serving plate and cover the surface of each one with the blended beans, followed by your favourite salsas and sauce or sauces. Top with some some rocket leaves and finish with the sliced beef. Enjoy!

Note *Traditional tlayudas are extra big, but it is best to start slowly, learning how to make them with smaller amounts of dough. Start with a 40 g/1½ oz. piece of dough, then gradually work up to making them bigger using 70 g/2¾ oz.*

VERACRUZ-STYLE PICADITAS
PICADITAS VERACRUZANAS

*Picaditas are quite similar to Sopecitos (see page 68), but this one is from
a different area in Mexico and is served here with wilted pumpkin flowers.*

500 g/1 lb. 2 oz. nixtamalized
  corn dough (see page 26)
1 tablespoon salt
240 ml/1 cup water if needed

TO SERVE
Red Sauce or Green Sauce
  (see page 25)
8 pumpkin flowers, slightly wilted
½ white onion, finely chopped
1 cup grated/shredded fresh
  cheese (such as feta, ricotta
  or *quesa fresca*)

SERVES 4

Preheat a large, dry frying pan/skillet over a medium heat.

Take a ball of corn dough roughly the size of your fist, work it briefly in your hands, then shape it into a fat tortilla about 5–8 mm/¼–½ inch thick. Cook the tortilla for about 1 minute on one side, then flip and cook for about 2 minutes on the other side, before flipping again. Pinch the edges of the tortilla to make a picadita with raised sides to contain the sauce. Continue to cook the picaditas for a further 5–6 minutes, flipping it a couple more times to make sure the dough is cooked properly or until it is a bit crispy outside and starts to take on some colour. Repeat with the rest of the dough.

Arrange the picaditas on a serving plate and top with a spoonful of your favourite red or green sauce and the wilted pumpkin flowers. Finish with some onion and cheese.

TAMALES
TAMALES

There are lots of ways to prepare the dough for tamales used across Mexico. But I find this method a very easy way to make the perfect tamal without too many complications.

15–18 dry corn husks (leaves), soaked in warm water for 1 hour (see Note below)
filling of your choice
sauce of your choice

BASIC TAMAL DOUGH
150 g/5½ oz. duck fat
1 tablespoon salt
500 g/1 lb. 2 oz. nixtamalized corn dough (see page 26)

MAKES ABOUT 8–10 TAMALES

Note I have suggested more corn husks/leaves here than you need. Some of them can be very small and you may be able to make more than the 10 tamales suggested. I use the rest of the leaves to cover the tamales during the steaming process.

HOW TO MAKE THE BASIC TAMAL DOUGH
Mix the duck fat and salt in a food processor or in a large bowl. Add the nixtamalized corn dough and blend together until smooth. The dough should taste a bit salty.

HOW TO FOLD THE TAMALES
Remove the corn husk leaves from the water and let them dry off for a few minutes.

Place one leaf on the work surface/counter top and using your hand spread 1 heaped tablespoonful of the tamal dough (about 60 g/2 oz.) over the wider top part of the leaf.

Top with about 60 g/2 oz. of filling and any sauce if using (see the individual recipes on the following pages for flavour variations).

Use the outer edges of the leaf to fold the sides of the dough over the filling, enclosing it in the dough.

Fold the leaf so that it overlaps the filling and its edges, enclosing everything.

Gently push the filling up inside the corn leaf if needed, then fold the bottom edge up and over to make a neat parcel.

Use a narrow strip of one of the spare corn leaves to securely tie the bottom edge of the parcel if liked.

Use a second strip of a spare corn leaf to tie the parcel at the top end, gathering the leaf at the top and tying it tightly.

Repeat until all of the tamales have been prepared.

Preheat a steamer (*tamalera*). Add all the tamales, standing them upright in the steamer with the top end facing upwards. Lay any spare corn leaves that you have on top and leave to steam for 60 minutes over a medium heat. Serve straight away.

BEAN TAMALES
TAMALES DE FRIJOL

This tamal is probably one of the first combinations that people made in Central Mexico. It is very simple but with the right seasoning it is an amazing version to share with friends.

1 quantity of Basic Tamal Dough
   (see page 102)
15–18 dry corn husks (leaves),
   soaked in warm water for 1 hour
   (see Note below)
Red Sauce or Green Sauce
   (see page 25), to serve

OAXACA-STYLE BEANS
500 g/2 cups pinto beans, rinsed
1 white onion, cut in half
½ garlic bulb
1½ teaspoons hoja santa powder
1½ teaspoons avocado leaf powder
120 ml/½ cup olive oil
sea salt

MAKES ABOUT 10 TAMALES

To prepare the beans, soak the beans in plenty of water overnight, then drain and discard the water.

Place the soaked beans in a saucepan with the onion, garlic and some salt and cover with water. Cook for 1–2 hours or until they are cooked and soft. Remove and discard the onion and garlic, then transfer the cooked beans to a food processor and blend with the hoja santa and avocado powders until smooth. Pass through a fine-mesh sieve/strainer to make an even smoother. Heat the oil in a saucepan over a medium heat. Add the blended beans and cook for about 15 minutes. Taste and adjust the seasoning if needed.

Make the tamales following the instructions on page 102, topping the dough with about 60 g/2 oz. of the bean mixture before folding. Repeat until all the tamales have been prepared.

Cook the tamales following the instructions on page 102.

Serve straight away with your favourite red or green sauce.

Note These tamales could also be served with some crumbled fresh cheese on top or grated/shredded Grana Padano.

PORK TAMALES
TAMALES DE CERDO

*This tamal is very well known all over Mexico, you will find
it at almost every tamal stall and can be made with a variety of fillings.*

1 quantity of Basic Tamal Dough
   (see page 102)
15–18 dry corns husk (leaves),
   soaked in warm water for 1 hour
500 ml/2 cups Green Sauce
   (see page 25), to serve

PORK FILLING
1 kg/2¼ lb. pork shoulder,
   cut into 5-cm/2-in. cubes
1 onion
1 garlic bulb
1 tablespoon sea salt

MAKES ABOUT 10 TAMALES

Cook the pork in a saucepan with the onion, garlic, salt and
3 litres/ 3 quarts water for about 1 hour or until the meat is really
soft. Remove and discard the onion and garlic and use 2 forks to
shred the meat. Set aside the shredded meat in a bowl until needed.

Make the tamales following the instructions on page 102, topping
the dough with about 60 g/2 oz. of the shredded pork meat and
3 tablespoons of the green sauce before folding. Repeat until all
the tamales have been prepared.

Cook the tamales following the instructions on page 102. Serve
straight away.

CHICKEN TAMALES
TAMALES DE SALSA ROJA CON POLLO

This is not a common tamal, but is a good alternative to red meat.

1 quantity of Basic Tamal Dough
   (see page 102)
15–18 dry corn husk (leaves),
   soaked in warm water for 1 hour

CHICKEN FILLING
150 ml/⅔ cup olive oil
1 onion, finely chopped
3 garlic cloves, finely chopped
3 jalapeño, finely chopped
500 g/1 lb. 2 oz. boneless chicken
   thighs, chopped
500 g/1 lb. 2 oz. tomatoes,
   blended
2 teaspoons chopped fresh
   coriander/cilantro
salt and black pepper

MAKES ABOUT 10 TAMALES

Heat the oil in a saucepan over a medium heat and cook the onion,
garlic and jalapeño for about 1 minute. Add the chicken and some
salt and cook for about 1 minute. Add the tomatoes, coriander,
salt and black pepper and cook for a further 10 minutes. Shred
the chicken in the sauce before using.

Make the tamales following the instructions on page 102, topping
the dough with about 80 g/½ oz. of the chicken mixture before
folding. Repeat until all the tamales have been prepared.

Cook the tamales following the instructions on page 102. Serve
straight away.

*Note You could also add some cheese along with the chicken
before closing the tamales.*

MUSHROOM TAMALES
TAMALES DE HONGOS

*This recipe is inspired by the ingredients found in central Mexico that
I grew up surrounded by and now use extensively in my restaurant.*

1 quantity of Basic Tamal Dough
  (see page 102)
15–18 dry corn husks (leaves),
  soaked in warm water for 1 hour

MUSHROOM FILLING
150 ml/⅔ cup olive oil
1 onion, finely chopped
3 garlic cloves, finely chopped
1 jalapeño, finely chopped (use the
  seeds if you want more heat)
500 g/1 lb. 2 oz. mixed
  mushrooms (I love chanterelles
  or a mix of wild mushrooms, but
  you can use your favourite type)
500 g/1 lb. 2 oz. tomatoes,
  blended (you can use a good-
  quality passata here if you can't
  get hold of ripe tomatoes)
2 teaspoons chopped fresh parsley
sea salt, to taste

MAKES ABOUT 10 TAMALES

Heat the oil in a saucepan over a medium heat and cook the onion, garlic and jalapeño for about 1 minute. Add the mushrooms and salt and cook for about 10 minutes. Add the tomatoes and parsley and cook for a further 10 minutes.

Make the tamales following the instructions on page 102, topping the dough with about 100 g/3½ oz. of the mushroom mixture before folding. Repeat until all the tamales have been prepared.

Cook the tamales following the instructions on page 102. Serve straight away.

MAIN DISHES
PLATOS PRINCIPALES

t happened more often on weekends, but really, any day of the week, lunch in my family could be quite a reunion of aunts, uncles, grandma, cousins and friends — besides my sister and my mother. Many family conflicts were resolved around the lunch table. It is the moment when families catch up, make plans and get the latest news (or gossip). The custom of eating together as a family is very much widespread in Mexico.

Lunch in Mexico happens in the afternoon, around 3pm or 4pm, and it's a dynamic affair. Everything is laid on the table at once: perhaps one or two main dishes, plus rice, beans, salsas, avocado slices, wedges of lemon or lime, chopped veggies like raw onion, fresh coriander/cilantro, cucumber, radishes, and of course, lots of warm tortillas in a basket lined with a special cloth or dish towel, and everyone serving themselves. Even if I was upset with my mum or my sister, I would have to talk to them, only if to ask them to pass the tortillas.

Some of the recipes in this chapter were staples growing up. The Mexican-style Courgettes (see page 122) is one of my favourite dishes — and it is vegetarian. Mexicans used to be more plant-based; before the conquest, historians tell us that the Mesoamerican diet was mainly vegetarian, although they did consume animal protein from fish, birds, domesticated turkeys and dogs, and insects. But still nowadays, my country is a paradise for vegetarians, with a vibrant and wide variety of fresh greens, mushrooms, pulses/legumes, seeds and the pervasive corn in its many forms.

From our Mexican ancestors also comes the widespread use of tomato-chilli-onion based sauces. In fact, the word molli, from which mole derives, means 'sauce' in Nahuatl. Along with the comal, the blender is probably the most used tool in the Mexican kitchen, doing the work that used to be done with a molcajete (a mortar) or the metate (a more powerful tool used to grind corn) to create the moles that enliven every meal.

A mole can be very simple, and it does not necessarily contain cacao. A very common misconception outside of Mexico is that moles always contain chocolate and many other ingredients. And some of them do, like the Poblano mole and some Oaxacan ones. These complex sauces with more than twenty ingredients were invented and perfected in convents and in the houses of rich criollos, and they were not consumed every day. Still now, these moles are eaten during weddings and parties.

Adobos, or marinades, are also widespread in Mexican home cooking. These follow the same basic principles of moles: varying combinations of tomatoes, onions, garlic, herbs, spices and chillies/chiles are blended and diluted sometimes in vinegar, sometimes in fruit juice, to marinate fish, poultry or meat.

Depending on the recipe and the preference of every cook, the ingredients for adobos and moles might be lightly charred over an open flame, or toasted on the comal, or fried before blending, or you can blend them raw and cook them afterwards, much like they do in India. Here in this chapter, you have examples of several techniques: for mole verde (see page 125), you cook all the ingredients for the sauce and then blend them; for the slow-cooked birria (see page 121), you blend them first and then cook it with the meat; the marinade or adobo for tikin xic (see page 133) calls for a mixture of roasted and raw ingredients.

There are a few soups or soupy stews in this chapter. We love soups in Mexico, and if they are hearty and nourishing, these can often become the main lunch dish. Make up some different agua fresca (see pages 157–8) and some fresh tortillas to go with the soup, and you will be recreating a typical everyday Mexican lunch. To look like a true Mexican, you will need to add a bit of salt to the tortilla, roll it like a cigar and then dunk it in your soup.

(From top left clockwise) Chile tabiche in Ocotlán, Oaxaca; tomatoes, onion, garlic and chillies/chiles that have been toasted in a pan until charred all over (see asada definition on page 188); hanging corn over an open grill; dried chillies, coriander/cilantro, cumin and ginger ready to be made into a broth; Cochinita pibil (see page 129).

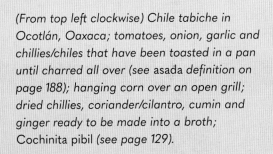

MUSHROOM ATAPAKUA

ATAPAKUA DE HONGOS

Atapakua is a thick broth, originally from Michoacán, that can be made with any vegetable, herb, fish or meat. The main characteristic of this recipe is that the broth is thickened with corn dough or fresh corn.

150 ml/⅔ cups vegetable oil
½ white onion, finely chopped
370 g/4 cups mushrooms, cleaned and cut in half or in 4 pieces if they are big
2 pinches of freshly ground black pepper
2 pinches of salt
pinch of avocado leaf powder

SAUCE
340 g/2 cups fresh corn kernels
200 ml/scant 1 cup vegetable oil
¼ white onion, roughly chopped
2 garlic cloves, roughly chopped
3 tablespoons pumpkin seeds
3 guajillo chillies/chiles, seeds and veins removed
2 tomatoes, seeds removed and roughly chopped
½ tablespoon avocado leaf powder
1½ tablespoons salt

TO SERVE
cooked beans or rice (optional)
warm tortillas (see page 26)

SERVES 2

Cook the corn kernels in a small saucepan of water and a pinch of salt. Drain the corn, reserving the cooking water. Set aside 1 cup of the corn to use as a garnish.

First, make the sauce. Heat the oil in a saucepan over a medium-high heat. Add the onion and garlic and cook until browned. Add the pumpkin seeds and chillies and cook for 1 minute, then add the tomatoes and cook, stirring, for a further 5 minutes. Take the pan off the heat and leave the sauce to cool down a bit.

Transfer the sauce to a food processor or blender with the reserved corn cooking water, avocado leaf powder and the salt and blend until smooth. Pass through a fine-mesh sieve/strainer for an even smoother sauce. Set aside until needed.

Heat the oil in a saucepan over a medium-high heat. Add the onion and cook for about 5 minutes or until translucent. Add the mushrooms, season with the black pepper, salt and avocado leaf powder and cook for about 5 minutes. Reserver a small amount of the mushrooms to use as a garnish.

Add the blended sauce to the pan and bring to the boil. Taste and adjust the seasoning if necessary. Add more water if the broth is too thick.

Ladle the broth into bowls and top with the reserved corn kernels and mushrooms. Serve the broth with warm tortillas and a side of beans or rice if liked.

BEEF BROTH
CHURIPO

There are many different ways to cook this dish – with or without chilli/chile, some people add xoconostle (a type of pickling pear) or different vegetables like chickpeas/garbanzo beans, carrots, potatoes and cabbage. This broth is usually accompanied by corundas rather than the usual tortillas.

1 kg/2¼ lb. beef shin on the bone
2 tablespoons rock salt
1 white onion
1 whole garlic bulb, cut in half
140 g/1 cup cooked chickpeas/
  garbanzo beans (see Note
  below)
2 potatoes, left unpeeled and
  cut into small chunks
2 carrots, left unpeeled and
  cut into chunks
¼ small cabbage, cut into chunks
corundas (see page 86), to serve

SERVES 6

Fill a large saucepan with 2.5 litres/10 cups water and add the meat and salt. Place over a high heat and bring to the boil. Skim off any foam that rises to the surface as it boils. Turn the heat down to medium and add the onion, garlic and chickpeas. Cook for about 2–3 hours or until the meat is falling off the bone.

Add the potatoes and carrots and cook for 5–10 minutes until they are tender. Add the cabbage, then turn off the heat. Taste and adjust the seasoning if needed. Serve immediately. with corundas on the side.

Notes

You can use canned chickpeas, but I always prefer to use dried ones, that are soaked and cooked before using. I prefer to know that I am using the most natural ingredients, which are free from preservatives.

If you want to make a churipo with chilli/chile, blend 4 deseeded and deveined guajillo chillies with some of the broth, then strain and add the blended chillies to the broth when you are about to start cooking the potatoes.

TLALPEÑO-STYLE BROTH

CALDO TLALPEÑO

This restorative broth is perfect for when you are recovering from a cold or just feeling generally run down. It is a strong broth with lots of flavour. You can also adjust the chilli/chile content to make it as spicy as you wish.

1 whole chicken, cut into 10 pieces, cleaned and patted dry
½ white onion
½ garlic bulb
2 fresh bay leaves
2 tablespoons rock salt
140 g/1 cup cooked chickpeas/garbanzo beans
3 fresh corn-on-the-cob/ears of corn, cut into 3 pieces
2 potatoes, peeled and cut into chunks
2 carrots, peeled and chopped
3 tomatoes, chopped
1 x 200-g/7-oz. can of chipotle in adobo (how much you add depends on how spicy you like your broth, see Note below)
2 courgettes/zucchini, cut into chunks

TO SERVE
lime wedges
finely chopped onion
avocado slices
fresh cheese, grated/shredded or crumbled

SERVES 8

Fill a large saucepan with 2.5 litres/10 cups water. Add the chicken pieces and bring to the boil. Skim off any foam that rises to the surface as it boils. Lower the heat, then add the onion, garlic, bay leaves, salt and chickpeas.

After about 30 minutes, or once the chicken is almost cooked, add the fresh corn pieces, potato chunks, carrots, tomatoes and canned chipotles and cook for about 10 minutes.

Once the chicken is soft and the potatoes are tender, add the courgettes and bring to the boil again. Turn off the heat – I don't like to let it boil for too long as the vegetables will be overcooked. Taste the broth before serving and adjust the seasoning if needed.

You can either serve the broth in bowls with the whole pieces of chicken, or you can remove the chicken, shred the meat, then add it back in before serving.

Serve the bowls of broth with lime wedges on the side and some finely chopped onion, avocado slices and fresh cheese for people to add their own toppings as liked.

Note I sometimes use dried chipotles instead of canned. I simply rehydrate them in warm water, remove the seeds and veins (they are quite spicy) and blend them with a bit of the chicken stock. I add the blended chipotles little by little, until the broth is just spicy enough. Another option is to add one or two whole chipotles directly to the broth, to let the flavours infuse – just be careful if you try to eat them, as they will be spicy.

NORTHERN-STYLE BEEF STEW
BIRRIA

This is one of the most well-known dishes from Jalisco, where it is usually made with mutton, goat, beef, chicken or fish. The traditional technique for cooking birria *is similar to the* barbacoa *(see page 188), cooking the meat with agave leaves called* pencas. *There are many different ways to cook* birria *and some other ways to serve it, but this is an easy method for beginners.*

2 kg/2¼ lb. beef shin or lamb shoulder, cut into 10-cm/4-in. chunks with the bones left in
1½ tablespoons salt
sea salt

SAUCE
10 guajillo chillies/chiles, seeds and veins removed and lightly toasted
4 cascabel or pasilla chillies/chiles, seeds and veins removed and lightly toasted
4 anchos chillies/chiles, seeds and veins removed and lightly toasted
7 garlic cloves
½ white onion, cut into chunks
1 tablespoon cumin seeds
½ tablespoon black peppercorns
4 cloves
1 tablespoon Mexican dried oregano
2 tablespoons white wine vinegar
2 kg/2¼ lbs. tomatoes, asados (see page 188), seeds and skins removed (optional)

TO SERVE
warm tortillas (see page 26)
your favourite salsas and sauces (see pages 19–25)

SERVES 10

First, prepare the sauce. Place all the ingredients for the sauce in a food processor or blender with 500 ml/2 cups water and blend until smooth. Strain through a fine-mesh/strainer for an even smoother sauce. In Mexico, we add water to the pulp left in the sieve and then strain again to extract maximum flavour.

Preheat the oven to 200°C/180°C fan/400°/Gas 6.

Season the meat with salt and place in a deep roasting pan. Roast in the preheated oven for about 10 minutes or until the meat starts to take on some colour. Pour the sauce over the meat, making sure that everything is covered — if there is not enough sauce to cover the meat, add a bit more water. Lower the oven temperature to 180°C/160°C fan/350°F/Gas 4. Cover the roasting pan with kitchen foil and cook for 4–5 hours until the meat easily falls off the bone.

Serve the birria with tortillas and your favourite salsas and sauces.

Notes
For a deeper flavour, marinate the meat in the sauce for an entire day before cooking.

Another way to cook the birria is on the hob/stove in a medium saucepan, similar to a broth or soup.

MEXICAN-STYLE COURGETTES

CALABACITAS A LA MEXICANA

This recipe is a really good vegetarian option. It can be served as a main dish with tortillas and sour cream or as a side with grilled steak or chicken.

4 tablespoons olive oil
½ white onion, finely chopped
1 garlic clove, finely chopped
1 corn-on-the-cob/ears of corn, kernels removed
1 tablespoon sea salt
6 tomatoes, cut into small cubes
2 pinches of Mexican dried oregano
1 kg/2¼ lb. courgettes/zucchini, cut into 1-cm/⅓-in. cubes
20 g/½ cup finely chopped fresh coriander/cilantro

SERVES 4

Heat the oil in a saucepan over a medium heat. Add the onion and cook for about 5 minutes. Add the garlic and cook for about 3 minutes, stirring continuously.

Add the corn kernels, season with the salt and cook for 5 minutes. Add the tomatoes and cook for 10 minutes. Add the oregano and courgettes and cook for a further 10 minutes.

Finally, add the coriander. Taste and adjust the seasoning if needed. Serve immediately with warm tortillas and sour cream on the side.

MUSHROOM TESMOLE

TESMOLE DE HONGOS

This delicious dish can be found in the states of Tlaxcala, Puebla, Veracruz and Estado de Mexico. It is a light mole blended with corn dough to make it thicker. I recommend serving with tortillas and finely chopped parley on top.

1 litre/4 cups vegetable or chicken stock
4 guajillo chillies/chiles, seeds removed
½ white onion, finely chopped
2 tomatoes
2 garlic cloves, finely chopped
pinch of freshly ground black pepper
pinch of Mexican dried oregano
120 g/½ cup nixtamalized corn dough (see page 26)
2 tablespoons vegetable oil
140 g/2 cups fresh mushrooms, chopped
salt

SERVES 2

Place half the stock in a saucepan over a high heat. Add the chillies, onion, tomatoes and garlic and bring to the boil. Continue to cook over a medium heat for about 20 minutes.

Transfer to a food processor or blender and blitz until smooth Pass through a fine-mesh sieve/strainer for an even smoother texture.

Wipe out the processor or blender and blend the remaining stock with a pinch of salt and the black pepper, oregano and corn dough.

Heat the oil in a saucepan over a medium heat and cook the mushrooms until they start to take on a bit of colour. Add the blended chilli mixture and bring to the boil.

Add the blended corn dough mixture. Use a whisk to mix everything together. Whisk continuously until the mixture starts to boil. Taste and adjust the seasoning if needed. Serve immediately.

ROAST CHICKEN WITH GREEN MOLE

MOLE VERDE O PIPIÁN CON POLLO

A green mole from the central area in Mexico, which is given its distinctive bright green colour through the use of fresh green herbs.

1 whole chicken (1.2–1.4 kg/ 2¼–2 lb. 6 oz.), spatchcocked

MARINADE
½ white onion
3 garlic cloves
bunch of fresh coriander/cilantro
bunch of fresh parsley
½ jalapeño, seeds removed
50 ml/3½ tablespoons olive oil

GREEN MOLE
250 ml/1 cup olive oil
1 white onion, chopped
5 garlic cloves, chopped
1 kg/2¼ lb. poblano chillies/chiles (about 8 chillies), skin and seeds removed (see Note below)
1 tablespoon cumin seeds, lightly toasted
1 tablespoon black peppercorns, lightly toasted
2 fresh bay leaves
250 g/3½ cups pumpkin seeds
1 kg/2¼ lbs. tomatillos, husks removed and cut into quarters
1 litre/4 cups chicken stock
2 tablespoons sea salt
200 g/7 oz. fresh coriander/ cilantro
200 g/7 oz. fresh parsley
150 g/5½ oz. fresh mint

TO SERVE
white rice
warmed tortillas (see page 26)
grilled/broiled or blanched green vegetables (such as fine beans)

SERVES 4

First, make the marinade. Put all the ingredients for the marinade and 100 ml/scant ½ cup water in a food processor or blender and blitz until smooth. Place the chicken on a plate. Rub the marinade all over the chicken, ensuring it is well coated. Cover and leave to marinate overnight in the fridge.

Preheat the oven to 180°C/160°C fan/350°F/Gas 4 or prepare the barbecue. Place the chicken on a lined baking sheet and roast in the preheated oven for about 30–45 minutes depending on the size of the chicken or cook on a hot grill, skin side down first, then turn over to continue cooking.

Meanwhile, make the green mole. Heat the oil in a saucepan over a medium heat. Add the onion and garlic and cook for 5 minutes or until they just start to colour. Add the poblano chillies and cook for about 5 minutes. Add all the spices, bay leaves and pumpkin seeds and cook for 5 minutes. Add the tomatillos, stock and salt and cook for a further 15 minutes. Taste to check the seasoning, adding more salt if needed.

Stir in the fresh herbs, then transfer everything to a food processor and blend to a smooth sauce. Pass through a fine-mesh sieve/strainer for an even smoother sauce.

Spoon the green mole into a serving dish and serve it with the chicken pieces, rice, tortillas and some grilled/broiled or blanched green vegetables.

Notes
To remove the skin from a chilli/chile or pepper, carefully hold the chilli over hot coals or an open flame until the skin has charred all over. Leave to cool, then peel away the charred skin.

If you want to increase the level of spice in this dish, you can also add a jalapeño that has been quartered when you add the other chillies to the green mole.

In Mexico, traditionally the chicken would be boiled in a large saucepan of water with some onion and garlic, but roasting it in the oven or on a hot barbecue gives a great flavour.

CHICKEN STEW

TINGA

This recipe is typically served each year on 16th September as part of the Mexican Independence Day celebrations but it is also enjoyed as a daily meal. Some people use canned chillies/chiles, however I prefer to use dried chillies/chiles for their smoky flavour.

60 ml/¼ cup vegetable oil

2 white onions, thinly sliced

3 garlic cloves, finely chopped

1.2 kg/2¾ lb. tomatoes, blended and strained

2 tablespoons salt

60 ml/¼ cup chipotle paste see Note below)

6 whole allspice berries

1 teaspoon freshly ground black pepper

6 fresh bay leaves

800 g/1¾ lb. cooked and shredded chicken breast

240 ml/1 cup chicken stock or water

TO SERVE

tostadas (see page 29)

fresh cheese

sour cream

finely chopped iceberg lettuce

any of your favourite spicy salsas and sauces (see page 19–25)

SERVES 8

Heat the oil in a saucepan over a medium-high heat. Add the onions and cook for 5 minutes or until translucent. Add the garlic and cook for about 2 minutes or until they start to take on some colour. Add the strained tomatoes, salt, chipotle paste, allspice berries, black pepper and bay leaves. Cook for about 5 minutes, stirring every couple of minutes, then lower the heat and add the shredded chicken and stock or water. Cook for another 10 minutes. Taste and add more salt if needed. Simmer for a further 10 minutes.

Serve the stewed chicken on top of tostadas with fresh cheese, sour cream, lettuce and one or two spicy salsas and sauces.

Notes

To make your own chipotle paste, blend a 200-g/7-oz. can of chipotles in adobo (available from online stockists) in a food processor or blender. Just be careful when adding it to the stew if you don't like too much spice.

You can also use the chicken stew as the filling for quesadillas (see page 93).

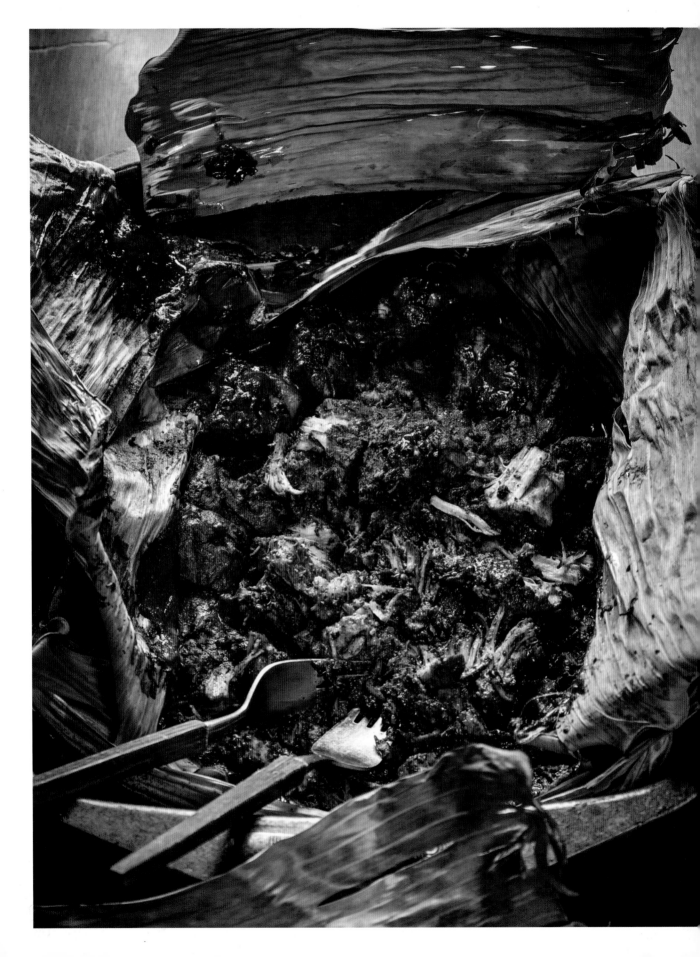

PIBIL-STYLE PORK
COCHINITA PIBIL

Cochinita pibil *is a very popular dish from the Yucatán peninsula. The Mayan word 'pib' refers to a traditional oven dug underground in which people cook a cochinita (suckling pig) in this region of Mexico.*

1 kg/2¼ lb. pork leg, cut into chunks
500 g/1 lb. 2 oz. banana leaves, *asados* (see Note below)
warmed tortillas and rice, to serve

MARINADE
200 g/7 oz. axiote paste
500 ml/2 cups freshly squeezed orange juice (from about 8–10 oranges)
½ white onion, cut into 3 pieces
3–4 garlic cloves
3 fresh bay leaves
1 teaspoon allspice berries, ground to a powder in a mortar and pestle (*molcajete*)
50 ml/3½ tablespoons white wine vinegar
salt

HABANERO & ONION PICKLE
1 red onion, thinly sliced
1 habanero chilli/chile, thinly sliced with seeds left in
250 ml/1 cup white wine vinegar
1 tablespoon salt
1 teaspoon Mexican dried oregano

SERVES 6–8

To make the marinade, place all the ingredients in a food processor and blend together until smooth.

Put the pork chunks into a large bowl and pour over the marinade. Turn the pork in the marinade to make sure that the meat is well coated, then cover and refrigerate overnight to marinate.

To make the habanero and onion pickle, combine all the ingredients in a bowl and leave for about 1 hour to infuse before serving.

Preheat the oven to 200°C/180°C fan/400°F/Gas 6.

Line a deep roasting pan with the banana leaves, leaving the long edges hanging over each side to cover the meat completely once in the pan. Spoon the marinated pork on top of the banana leaves. Fold the long edges of the banana leaves over the top of the pork, ensuring that the meat is covered and sealed inside the leaves.

Roast in the preheated oven for 1 hour or until the pork is cooked and juicy. Taste the meat before taking it out of the oven to make sure is properly cooked.

Use 2 forks to shred the meat, mixing it with all the juices in the pan. Taste and adjust the seasoning if needed.

Serve the shredded pork in warmed tortillas with the habanero sauce and rice.

Notes
Asados means that the banana leaves need to be scorched quickly over an open flame or with a blowtorch before using (see page 188 for a full explanation).

You can also serve with a Red Sauce (see page 25) or your favourite Mexican sauce as preferred.

VERACRUZ-STYLE FISH

PESCADO A LA VERACRUZANA

The vast variety of fish available in Mexico makes this recipe a very popular and delicious dish. It is quite Mediterranean in style, and is one of the richest and most complex sauces in Veracruz.

4–6 cod or sea bass fillets (each weighing at least 150 g/5½ oz.), skin on
120 ml/½ cup olive oil
4 fresh thyme sprigs
salt and freshly ground black pepper
2 tablespoons chopped fresh parsley, to garnish

TOMATO PURÉE
9 tomatoes
2 garlic cloves
¼ white onion

SAUCE
80 ml/⅓ cup olive oil
¼ white onion, finely chopped
3 garlic cloves, finely chopped
7 tomatoes, blanched in hot water, skins and seeds removed and flesh diced
3 bay leaves
1 tablespoon Mexican dried oregano
½ tablespoon dried thyme, crushed
1 tablespoon fresh marjoram
1 tablespoon freshly ground black pepper
3 pickled yellow chillies/chiles
50 g/1¾ oz. pitted/stoned green olives
50 g/1¾ oz. capers in brine, drained
50 g/¼ cup pickled jalapeños
1 teaspoon pickled jalapeño juice
450 g/1 lb. baby potatoes, peeled and boiled

SERVES 4–6

First, prepare the tomato purée. Cook the tomatoes in a saucepan with 240 ml/1 cup water for about 20 minutes. Transfer to a food processor or blender with the garlic and onion and blend together. Pass through a fine-mesh sieve/strainer for an even smoother purée.

Next, make the sauce. Heat the olive oil in a saucepan over a medium heat. Add the onion and cook for about 2 minutes, then add the garlic. Once they start to colour, add the diced tomatoes, blended tomato purée, herbs and spices. Cook for about 15 minutes.

Add the olives, capers, pickled jalapeños, jalapeño juice and potatoes. Leave to simmer for about 10 minutes.

Season the fish with salt and pepper. Heat the olive oil in a large frying pan/skillet over a medium heat. Place the fish in the pan, skin side down, along with the thyme. Once the skin starts to take on some colour and the fish looks halfway cooked, flip the fish to finish cooking. Keep an eye on the thyme; if starts to burn, take it out.

Add some of the sauce to cook together with the fish for about 4–5 minutes, depending on the size of the fillets.

Carefully transfer the fish from the pan to serving plates and serve garnished with some chopped parsley leaves.

AXIOTE-MARINATED SEA BREAM
TIKIN XIC

On the Yucatán peninsula, traditionally people grill whole fish directly over hot coals. but some people do use their indoor ovens too. I have used responsibly sourced sea bream, but you could also try sea bass; in this region people usually use mero, huachinango or pámpano.

1 large or 2 medium sea bream or sea bass (about 800 g/ 1 lb. 12 oz.), butterflied and pin boned (you could ask a fishmonger to help with this)
2 banana leaves, blanched in hot water for 15 seconds to soften
salt and ground white pepper

AXIOTE MARINADE
200 g/7 oz. axiote paste
400 ml/1¾ cups freshly squeezed orange juice
¼ onion, asado (see page 188)
4 garlic cloves, asados
½ tablespoon ground allspice
2 cloves, toasted
25 ml/1½ tablespoons olive oil
1 fresh bay leaf
15 g/1 tablespoon sea salt
40 ml/2½ tablespoons white wine vinegar

FILLING
1 green (bell) pepper, thinly sliced
1 yellow (bell) pepper, thinly sliced
1 red (bell) pepper, thinly sliced
1 bunch of fresh coriander/ cilantro, finely chopped
2 pinches of sea salt
120 ml/½ cup olive oil

TO SERVE
fresh corn tortillas
avocado purée (see Note opposite)
lime wedges
Habanero Salsa (see page 19) or habanero and onion pickle (see page 129)

SERVES 2

First, make the marinade. Blend all the ingredients together in a food processor to a smooth paste. Rub the marinade all over the fish and season all over with salt and white pepper. Leave to marinate for about 1 hour.

To prepare the filling, combine all the ingredients in a bowl. Set aside until needed.

Preheat the oven to 180°C/160°C fan/350°F/Gas 4.

Line a deep roasting pan with the blanched banana leaves, leaving the long edges hanging over each side to cover the fish completely once in the pan.

Lay the fish on the banana leaves. Spoon the filling on top of the fish and add any leftover marinade. Fold the long edges of the banana leaves over the top of the fish, ensuring the fish is completely covered and sealed inside the leaves.

Bake in the preheated oven for about 30–40 minutes, depending on the size of the fish. To check if the fish is cooked, pull away a small piece of flesh to ensure it is cooked through.

Serve the fish wrapped in the banana leaves on a serving platter accompanied by fresh corn tortillas, avocado purée, plenty of lime wedges and either habanero salsa or habanero and onion pickle.

Note To make an avocado purée, simply blend 2 avocados, 50 g/ 1¾ oz. fresh coriander/cilantro, juice of 2 limes, 2 teaspoons sea salt, 50 ml/3½ tablespoons water and 50 ml/3½ tablespoons olive oil together in a food processor or blender. Taste and adjust the seasoning if needed. Pass through a fine-mesh sieve/strainer for an even smoother purée if liked.

CELEBRATIONS

CELEBRACIONES

n Mexico, there is always a big celebration around every corner. It can be a national holiday such as Independence Day on the 15th September, or it can be your niece's first birthday, but Mexicans need almost no excuse to call on guests, bring out the piñata, fill big tables with food and drinks and, of course, play music.

In this loud, brightly coloured country, celebrations are usually day-long affairs (or several days long in the case of weddings and funerals). Growing up in Mexico, I remember fondly many of these fiestas. Children's birthdays ended up with all the grown-ups drunk and dancing; lunch with friends often turns into dinner; weddings finish at dawn with the serving of chilaquiles (see page 42) and café de olla (see page 168). And many times, a live music band is hired (or several!). I have noticed foreigners' surprise at the extravagant lavishness that even the humblest family show to celebrate their daughter's quinciañera (15th birthday), a wedding or a special Day of the Dead. Mexicans 'throw everything out of the window' when it comes to sharing their joy.

It is no surprise that Christmas is one of the biggest celebrations in this (mostly) Catholic country. In Mexico, Christmas starts unofficially on the 12th December, the Day of Our Lady of Guadalupe, the patron virgin of Mexico. The complete holiday season lasts until the 6th January, the Día de Reyes (Epiphany Day), when children get their presents and families eat the Rosca de Reyes, a sweet brioche bread shaped like a ring. It is called the 'Guadalupe-Reyes Weekend', by far the longest 'weekend' of the year, and even though all the businesses remain open, things slow down considerably throughout the season.

During this time of the year, apart from Christmas Eve and New Year's Eve, people celebrate posadas, a unique Mexican tradition especially alive in smaller cities and towns. It used to be more popular in the past, and I remember

them growing up in Mexico City. Every night, from the 16th to the 23rd, several families host a reception in their homes to receive the 'pilgrims' who go around the town asking for posada (a place to stay). The pilgrims play out as Joseph and Mary in their journey from Nazareth to Bethlehem, and they hold candles and sing carols and litanies on the host's door until they are invited in.

My aunt and uncle used to organize a couple of posadas each year, and I remember being a pilgrim, or dressing up as the Virgin Mary and having a blast. It was all like a big theatre game for us kids, mostly interested in the costumes, the piñata and the delicious food: tamales, tostadas de pata (pork feet) or tinga (chicken stew), pambazos, buñuelos, churros — most of these things are fried, crunchy, sweet or savoury, or everything at once.

The tradition has many variations, but most posadas end up with the breaking a piñata filled with fruit and candy, and drinking ponche, a sweet concoction of spices, fruits and for the adults, spiked with alcohol, like tequila or mezcal.

Christmas Eve and New Year's Eve are both celebrated with family and friends around a beautiful table with plenty of food. In my own family, New Year's Eve was the big one, the time my extended family would come over. We would play games, break a piñata and wait for midnight to welcome the new year. We would always start with two classic Mexican Christmas dishes: romeritos, a seasonal green from Central Mexico cooked in a mole sauce with dried prawns/shrimp; and bacalao a la Vizcaína, a dish with Spanish roots made with salt cod and a tomato sauce with almonds, cinnamon, olives and other ingredients.

Some of these seemingly Catholic traditions have roots in pre-Columbian times. Often Mexicans would just move their celebrations a few days to coincide with the Christian calendar but kept their customs (like what food to eat or what colours to use). Two of the biggest celebrations in Mexico,

(From top left clockwise) Calenda (a type of street party) for a quinciañera in Oaxaca; Alebrije (Mexican folk art wood carvings) used during a street celebration; colourful paper decorating the streets of Oaxaca.

the Guadalupe pilgrimage and the Day of the Dead are mixed with pre Hispanic traditions.

Where the Guadalupe Basilica stands today in Mexico City, there used to be a temple dedicated to a female Aztec deity called Tonantzin ('our sacred mother' connected to the earth and fertility), and the custom to make a pilgrimage to this temple around the same time (early December) was already established when the Europeans came. Then as now, pilgrims came from far away to pay honour to this female deity that later became Our Lady of Guadalupe.

Mexicans also celebrated a festivity to honour the dead, which after colonization became entangled with the Christian All Saints Day in early November. Many elements of the celebration, such

as the tiered altars and the offering of food and drinks, are rooted in pre-Hispanic times and Mexican beliefs. For this celebration, people prepare the food that their deceased loved when they were alive, and leave dishes of it on the altar.

What is also purely Mexican is the festivities of the Day of the Dead. While in Christian countries this is a solemn celebration, in Mexico this is a happy, celebration of remembrance and reunion.

Growing up with all these traditions has left a mark on me. Now, as a Mexican living outside of my country for so long, I realize that what I learned is to celebrate life. It doesn't matter where, or for what reason, celebrating with friends and family is always important to me. It is a good way to honour life, and the people we love, alive or dead.

STUFFED PORK LEG

PIERNA MECHADA

This dish is really popular during the Christmas celebrations. My aunt used to cook it and we really love it. It requires a bit of attention and time, but I'm sure your family will enjoy it a lot once you've mastered the process.

2.5 kg/5½ lb. skinless pork leg
6 garlic cloves, peeled
12 whole black peppercorns
3 tablespoons sea salt
180 ml/¾ cup freshly squeezed orange juice
180 ml/¾ cup white wine
40 whole almonds, skinned and toasted
20 prunes, stoned/pitted and cut in half
20 streaky bacon rashers, cut into 2-cm/¾-in. pieces

ADOBO
6 guajillo chillies/chiles, seeds and veins removed and rehydrated in warm water
1 ancho chilli/chile, seeds and veins removed and rehydrated in warm water
4 morita chillies/chiles, seeds and veins removed and rehydrated in warm water
4 garlic cloves
2 tablespoons salt
pinch of cumin seeds
1 tablespoon dried Mexican oregano
6 whole allspice berries
2 pinches of dried thyme
2 tablespoons apple cider vinegar
2 bay leaves
1 tablespoon dark brown sugar

butchers' twine

SERVES 12

Make 5-cm/2-inch deep slits in the pork leg spaced about 5 cm/ 2 inches apart over the whole leg.

Use a mortar and pestle or a small blender to make a paste with the garlic, peppercorns and salt. Rub some of this paste into the slits made in the pork leg.

Mix the orange juice and wine in a large bowl and add the pork leg. Cover and place in the fridge overnight. This is really best prepared a whole day ahead, so you can leave it in the fridge, turning the leg every hour or so during the day, then leave it to fully marinate overnight if possible.

Blend all the ingredients for the adobo in a food processor or blender with 1 litre/4 cups water to as smooth a mixture as possible. You can add a bit of the chilli soaking water if the mixture is too thick. Pass through a fine-mesh sieve/strainer for an even smoother texture if liked. Set aside.

Take the leg out of the fridge 1 hour before starting to cook to bring to room temperature. Preheat the oven to 200°C/180°C fan/400°F/ Gas 6.

Remove the pork from the marinade, reserving the liquid, and place the leg on top of a large chopping board. Start to add the almonds, prunes and bacon pieces, pushing them into the slits in the meat. Try to get a mix of all three into each hole, if possible, for maximum flavour. Use some butchers' cotton twine to tie the leg (see opposite).

Transfer the leg to a deep roasting pan and pour the adobo all over it. Also pour the reserved orange and wine marinade into the tray. Cover the pan with kitchen foil and roast in the preheated oven for 50 minutes. Lower the oven temperature to 180°C/160°C fan/350°C/ Gas 4 and roast for a further 30–35 minutes per kg/2 lbs. Let the leg rest for 10 minutes before slicing and serving with Apple Salad (see opposite) and the Beetroot Salad (see page 143).

HOW TO TIE THE PORK LEG

Secure the twine. Make a slip knot on one end of the meat. This is the anchor for your twine. Using a slip knot to set the twine in place means you can adjust this knot's placement and tension at any point during the tying.

Make a series of loops or half hitch knots to cover the roast. Here's the real work of this technique: you'll pull a length of twine out away from your anchor and create a large, loose loop. Slide this loop over the roast and shimmy it up about an inch from your anchor knot. Then repeat for the length of the roast.

Tie the roast from end to end. Once your roast is tied around its width, run the twine down the length of the meat, securing it under the loops. Pull the twine so that it's taut around the meat, but not too tight that it squishes the roast. Secure the twine at your anchor knot and trim any excess. Now it's time to roast!

APPLE SALAD
ENSALADA DE MANZANA

**This salad is made especially for Christmas celebrations.
It is sort of like a Mexican version of a Waldorf salad.**

4 apples, cut into 1-cm/½-in. cubes (any yellow apple will work)
1 carrot, grated
100 g/½ cup cubed pineapple (fresh or canned)
4 tablespoons chopped pecan nuts, or more if you wish
360 ml/1½ cups sour cream
2 tablespoons caster/superfine sugar
pineapple juice, to taste (optional)

SERVES 4 AS A SIDE DISH

Place all the ingredients in a bowl and mix together well. If you feel the salad is a bit dry, I sometimes add a bit of pineapple juice.

Taste and add a bit more sugar if needed. Transfer to a nice serving bowl and top with some extra nuts to garnish.

Note You can add raisins instead of the extra nuts, if preferred.

MEXICAN TURKEY
PAVO RELLENO

This recipe is Barrocan in style and is normally served as part of the Christmas feast with the Stuffed Pork Leg (see page 138) and the salads in this chapter.

1 turkey weighing about 5–6 kg/ 11–13 lb.
450 g/4 sticks butter, cubed
1 apple
480 ml/2 cups freshly squeezed orange juice
240 ml/1 cup white wine

FILLING
200 ml/scant 1 cup olive oil
100 g/¾ stick unsalted butter
1 onion, finely chopped
3 garlic cloves, finely chopped
500 g/1 lb. 2 oz. minced/ground beef
500 g/1 lb. 2 oz. minced/ground pork
100 g/½ cup acitron (see note) or crystalized fruit, cubed
100 g/¾ cup black raisins
200 g/1½ cups stoned/pitted prunes, cut in half
100 g/1 cup stoned/pitted green olives, cut in half
130 g/1 cup blanched almonds, roughly chopped
2 apples, cubed
1 pear, cubed
115 g/1 cup pecan nuts, roughly chopped
2 red (bell) peppers, skins blackened, removed, chopped
120 ml/½ cup Jerez sherry
1 teaspoon ground cloves
½ tablespoon ground cinnamon
40 g/1 cup finely chopped fresh parsley
1 kg/2¼ lb. tomatoes, blended and strained
130 g/1 cup pine nuts
salt and black pepper

SERVES 8–10

Preheat the oven to 200°C/180°C fan/400°F/Gas 6.

First, prepare the filling for the turkey. Heat the oil and butter in a saucepan over a medium heat. Add the onion and garlic and cook until they start to take on colour. Add the minced beef and pork, season well with salt and black pepper and cook for 10 minutes, stirring continuously, so they mix together well.

Add the acitron or crystallized fruit, raisins and prunes, mix together and cook for about 3 minutes. Add the olives and almonds and cook for a further 3 minutes. Add the apples, pears, pecans, red pepper and sherry and keep stirring. Add the cloves, cinnamon and parsley, mix everything together and cook, stirring, for a further 5 minutes. Add the blended tomatoes and taste and adjust the seasoning if needed. Cook for another 10 minutes, then add the pine nuts and cook for a final 3 minutes. Taste, add more salt if needed, then take off the heat and leave to cool down.

Meanwhile, prepare the turkey. Smear the butter inside the turkey and sprinkle with salt and pepper.

Once the filling has cooled down slightly, press it into the turkey cavity and, once full, tie the legs together using string and finish with an apple between the legs.

Place the stuffed turkey in a deep roasting tray. Add more butter all over the turkey and pour over the orange juice and wine. Roast in the preheated oven, lower the temperature to 170°C/150°C fan/325°F/Gas 3 and cook for about 2 hours, checking every 10–15 minutes and basting with the juices to keep the turkey moist.

Serve straight away as part of your Christmas feast.

Notes

In Mexico, acitron used to be made with a cactus meat called biznaga, which is now in danger of extinction. Any kind of crystallized fruit peel, such as orange, can be used in its place though.

You may have more stuffing than you need, so it can be frozen for use on another occasion. Defrost thoroughly before using.

BEETROOT SALAD
ENSALADA DE BETABEL

The acidity content of this salad is quite high so it makes a really good side dish for the Stuffed Pork Leg (see page 138) that is also served at the Christmas dinner.

1 tablespoon honey
120 ml/½ cup freshly squeezed orange juice
3 tablespoons olive oil
3 cooked beetroots/beets, cut into cubes
2 oranges, peeled, pith removed and cut into segments
200 g/1½ cups jicama (also known as yam bean or Mexican potato), cut into cubes (replace with apples if you cannot find jicama)
180 g/1 cup cubed pineapple (fresh or canned)
50 g/½ cup roasted pecan nuts
65 g/½ cup roasted pine nuts
65 g/½ cup roasted peanuts
pinch of sea salt
rocket/arugula, to garnish

SERVES 4 AS A SIDE DISH

Place the honey, orange juice and olive oil in a large mixing bowl and mix together. Add the rest of the ingredients and mix together carefully. Once it is all combined, taste, and add more salt if needed. Transfer to a serving bowl and top with some rocket leaves to serve.

Note *You can also add raisins to this salad, if you like, but I usually leave them out.*

GRILLED MEAT TACOS
TACOS DE ASADA

This is the perfect dish for celebrating birthdays or special occasions, especially if it is a summer celebration and the meal can be cooked and enjoyed outdoors, cooking on a hot grill in the garden with friends and family, drinking beers. These tacos can be cooked on a hot charcoal grill – which is my favourite method – or in a large pan in the kitchen. Traditionally, the grilled meat is served with guacamole, beans, one or two spicy sauces (fresh or cooked), sometimes slices of radish or cucumber and tortillas, of course. There is no specific cut of meat for these tacos, so choose your favourite kind.

500 g/1 lb. 2 oz. rib-eye steak
500 g/1 lb. 2 oz. skirt steak or
   bavette
500 g/1 lb. 2 oz. rump steak
1 kg/2¼ lb. spring onions/scallions
sea salt

MARINADE
1 tablespoon freshly ground black
   pepper
½ teaspoon ground cloves
6 garlic cloves, finely chopped
½ tablespoon Mexican dried
   oregano
3 tablespoons apple cider vinegar
1 teaspoon ground cinnamon
2 tablespoons salt
120 ml/½ cup freshly squeezed
   orange juice

TO SERVE
warm tortillas (see page 26)
Avocado Salsa (see page 22)
Oaxaca-style Beans (see page 97)
any of your favourite rice dishes
   (see page 31)
any of your favourite spicy salsas
   and sauces (see pages 19–25)

SERVES 6

Place all the ingredients for the marinade in a bowl and mix together.

Place the meat in a large tray and pour over the marinade making sure all the meat is well coated. Leave in the fridge to marinate overnight. Take the meat out of the fridge 30 minutes before starting to cook to bring to room temperature.

When you are ready to cook, light the grill. Cook the spring onions for about 10 minutes until softened and starting to take on some colour.

Cook the meat on the hot grill. I like to cook my meat medium-rare for about 4 minutes on each side, but please cook to your liking. Alternatively, you can cook the meat in a hot pan over a high heat for the same timings.

Once the meat is ready, leave it to rest for about 2–3 minutes, then slice, season with salt and serve immediately with warm tortillas, avocado salsa, beans, rice and your favourite spicy salsas and sauces.

Notes
For the best results, ensure the meat is at room temperature before you start cooking it on the hot grill.

You can also check if the meat is cooked using a meat thermometer: for rare, around 52°C/125°F; for medium-rare, around 54°C/130°F; for medium-well, around 71°C/160°F; and for well done, around 74°C/165°F.

You can also cook any other vegetables that you would like at the same time as the spring onions/scallions – fresh corn, Tenderstem broccoli and asparagus all work well.

CHICKEN EN ADOBO

POLLO EN ADOBO

This is a very common dish served at birthday celebrations and is usually accompanied with nopales (cactus) that has also been cooked on the grill. I really enjoy cooking this type of recipe as the chicken carries lots of flavour. It is sometimes nice to prepare it on the weekend for a family gathering.

2 tablespoons vegetable oil
½ white onion, cut into chunks
3 garlic cloves, cut in half
6 tomatoes, quartered
8 guajillo chillies/chiles, seeds and veins removed
1 teaspoon ground cinnamon
2 bay leaves
1 teaspoon freshly ground black pepper
1½ tablespoons salt
360 ml/1½ cups chicken stock or water
2 tablespoons apple cider vinegar
6 chicken thighs, with or without bones

TO SERVE
any of your favourite rice dishes (see page 31)
warm tortillas (see page 26)
any of your favourite salsas and sauces (see pages 19–25)
salad

SERVES 4–6

Heat the vegetable oil in a saucepan over a medium-high heat. Add the onion and garlic and cook, stirring continuously. Once they start to take on some colour, add the tomatoes, chillies and spices, still stirring continuously. Continue to cook for 5 minutes, then add the stock or water and cook for a further 15 minutes. Lower the temperature slightly if needed and stir every 2–3 minutes. Leave to cool.

Place the cooled sauce in a food processor or blender with the vinegar and blend until smooth. Pass through a fine-mesh sieve/strainer for an even smoother adobo.

Marinate the chicken thighs in the blended adobo and leave in the fridge overnight. Take the meat out of the fridge 30 minutes before starting to cook to bring to room temperature.

I prefer to cook the chicken on a hot grill, but you can cook it in an oven preheated to 200°C/180°C fan/400°F/Gas 6 for about 40–50 minutes.

I recommend serving the chicken with rice, tortillas, your favourite sauce and a salad.

Note You may not need all of the adobo for marinating. You can keep the rest in a clean jar in the fridge for 4–5 days, or freeze for future use.

PRAWN TAMAL

TAMAL DE CAMARONES

During the holy week, people do not eat meat, so these kind of recipes are quite popular during this time. I recommend serving them with the Habanero Salsa (see page 19) and a little fresh salad made from mixed baby leaves topped with fresh coriander/cilantro.

500 g/1 bag banana leaves
1 quantity of Basic Tamal Dough
  (see page 102)

FOR THE FILLING
20 large raw prawns/shrimp,
  cleaned, shelled and deveined
4–6 tomatoes, seeds removed
  and cut into cubes
bunch of fresh coriander/cilantro,
  roughly chopped
1 small red onion, thinly sliced
480 ml/2 cups axiote marinade
  (see below)
salt

MAKES ABOUT 10 TAMALES

Take the banana leaves, cut 10 square leaves, about 25 cm/10 inches big, then soak them in a bowl of hot water for 2 minutes to soften. Remove from the water and pat them dry as well as possible.

Place one leaf in the palm of your hand and spread 1 heaped spoonful of tamal dough (60–80 g/2–3 oz.) on the leaf. Add 2 prawns, 1 tablespoon cubed tomatoes, some coriander, onion, a pinch of salt and 1½ tablespoons of the axiote marinade. Close and fold the tamal following the instructions on page 102, making sure the dough is enclosed. Continue with the rest of the ingredients.

Cook the tamales following the instructions on page 102. Serve straight away.

AXIOTE MARINADE

FOR THE MARINADE
200 g/7 oz. axiote paste
500 ml/2 cups freshly squeezed
  orange juice (from about 8–10
  oranges)
½ white onion
3–4 garlic cloves
3 fresh bay leaves
1 teaspoon allspice berries, ground
  to a powder in a mortar and
  pestle (*molcajete*)
50 ml/3½ tablespoons white wine
  vinegar
salt

To make the marinade, place all the ingredients in a food processor and blend together until smooth.

DRINKS
BEBIDAS

The following chapter on drinks encompasses morning beverages like traditional Mexican coffee and juices, hot drinks for special occasions like chocolate and fruit ponche, and also, my favourite cocktails, some of them made with tequila, mezcal and even *pox*, a cane-sugar and corn moonshine from the state of Chiapas that can now be found outside of that region. I have also included *aguas frescas* (flavoured waters) which are served everywhere in homes and restaurants, usually with lunch. They are so widespread in Mexico that when you go to a restaurant and want to drink plain water, you must specify you want 'simple water'. If you just ask for water, they will ask you: 'What flavour?'

Two of the most common *aguas* served are *horchata*, made with rice and cinnamon, and *agua de Jamaica con romero*, made with hibiscus flowers and sugar (see page 158). Tamarind water is another favourite (see page 157). You can make them with any fruit with a high water content like watermelon or mango; add herbs like basil or mint; chia seeds will give the water a thick texture, and you can even try adding nuts as I do in my recipe for melon and pecan water (see page 157). It is a great way to use up any piece of fruit that is about to go bad.

With this being a Mexican cookbook, I have included a chocolate drink that you can make with water or milk; you can also try adding chilli/chile powder and other spices, or use different types of milk. Mexicans did not keep cows before the 16th century, so they prepared their cacao drink with water and spices, and it was reserved for the higher class (cacao seeds were used as a currency). They did not distil any spirits, and their only alcoholic drinks were fermented ones. The most common alcoholic drink before the encounter with Europe was *pulque* – the fermented juice of some species of agave. People still drink this white, viscous liquid full of nutrients and healthy bacteria. But if you are not used to it, it can upset your stomach.

This takes us to the agaves, a large family of plants native to America with hundreds of species, also known as *magueyes*. Tequila and mezcal are both made with these amazing plants, which are used in Mexico for almost anything you can think of — their juice, to make medicine, their leaves, called *pencas*, are used for cooking, and the Otomí people from the state of Hidalgo still make fantastic looking roofs from them. The flowers can be eaten, as well as the cooked core of the plant, which is sweet and juicy and is where agave syrup comes from.

This sugary juice of the cooked agave core can be fermented and then distilled to make tequila, mezcal, raicilla, bacalora and many other agave moonshines. Tequila is both a destination of origin and a region, like Champagne, and all tequila is made with the blue agave plant (Agave tequilana), which lends itself to industrial-scale cultivation. Among the agaves, the blue one propagates easily and grows faster than other species.

Mezcal, however, is made in many other regions of Mexico, from different agaves, some of them wild, although Oaxacan mezcal stands out for its quality and variety. To make the most artisanal mezcal, the agave cores are cooked buried in the ground, the sweet cores are then smashed with stone mills to obtain the juice, which is distilled in earthenware stills. This kind of mezcal is now hard to find and expensive, even in Mexico.

The mezcal world exploded a few years ago, and now there are mezcal enthusiasts everywhere who want to try this elixir that seems to cure all ills. Mezcalerías, bars dedicated to mezcal, are now found not only in all major cities in Mexico but also in the US, Europe and Japan. The variety of mezcals is one of the characteristics that make this a unique drink. There are so many factors in its production that the results can be quite different, making it an endless universe of delicate flavours and sensations. So, let's raise our grateful glasses to Mayahuel, the goddess of the agave plant. ¡*Salud*!

(From top left clockwise) Tepeztate, one of the largest and longest lasting agaves; Maestro Mezcalero (mezcal maker) cutting and cleaning an agave heart – this agave is a papalometl; the rustic cooling process for the distillation; removing the agave having been cooked underground for 3 days; cow skin containers used to ferment mezcal.

JUICES
JUGO

VAMPIRE JUICE
VAMPIRO

This juice is really good for the blood circulation and contains good quantities of calcium, vitamins and minerals.

500 ml/2 cups freshly
   squeezed orange juice
240 ml/1 cup fresh carrot juice
240 ml/1 cup fresh beetroot/
   beet juice
juice of ½ lime
2 celery stalks with leaves, cleaned
   and cut into 4 pieces, to garnish

SERVES 3–4

Use a juicer to juice all the ingredients and mix together in a jug/pitcher. Serve straight away garnished with the celery stalks.

Note I made the fresh carrot and beetroot/beet juices with a small juicer machine, but another good option is a cold-press machine if you have one.

ANTI-FLU JUICE
ANTIGRIPAL

This fresh juice has a high vitamin C content and is good for the skin and to control stress.

500 ml/2 cups freshly
   squeezed orange juice
juice of 2 limes
6 strawberries
4 guavas, cut into 4 pieces
2 teaspoons honey

SERVES 2

Place all the ingredients in a blender and blitz until well combined and smooth. Serve straight away over ice if liked.

GREEN JUICE
VERDE

This juice is really good to start the day with. It contains a good quantity of fibre and antioxidants.

480 ml/2 cups freshly
   squeezed orange juice
170 g/1 cup roughly chopped
   fresh pineapple
1 lime, seeds removed and
   quartered
2 celeriac/celery root, roughly
   chopped
3 parsley sprigs with leaves,
   roughly chopped
pineapple leaves, to garnish
   (optional)

SERVES 2

Place all the ingredients in a blender and blitz until well combined and smooth. Serve straight away over ice if liked.

Clockwise from front: Vampire Juice, Green Juice and Anti-flu Juice.

FLAVOURED WATERS
AGUA FRESCAS

MELON & PECAN WATER

AGUA DE NUEZ Y MELÓN

Melons need to be very ripe for the best results here. These are two of my favourite ingredients, so I usually drink many glasses of this when it is on offer!

½ melon, flesh chopped
150 g/1¼ cups pecan halves
200 g/1 cup caster/superfine sugar

SERVES 6

Place the melon in a blender with 90 g/¾ cup of the pecans, the sugar and 500 ml/2 cups water and blitz together. Strain the mixture into a jug/pitcher and add another 500 ml/2 cups water. Chop the remaining pecans and add them to the jug. Enjoy over ice.

Note You can use 1 can of evaporated milk and 1 can of condensed milk as an alternative to the sugar if liked.

TAMARIND WATER

TAMARINDO

The slightly acidic flavour of the tamarind makes this water perfect to serve with meats. It also works well with grilled fish or prawns/shrimps.

200 g/7 oz. tamarind pulp
200 g/1 cup light brown sugar

SERVES 6

Place all the ingredients in a blender with 1 litre/4 cups water and blitz together. Strain the mixture into a jug/pitcher and add another 1 litre/4 cups water and some ice. Enjoy straight away.

Note You can use 250 g/9 oz. dried tamarind instead of tamarind pulp. This will need to be peeled and boiled in 1 litre/ 4 cups water. Leave this to rest for about 30 minutes and then blend with the sugar as above.

LEMON, MINT & CHIA WATER

AGUA DE LIMÓN CON CHIA

This recipe brings back a lot of memories from when I was little, especially of playing outside the house for hours on hot days, then coming back home and drinking a full glass of this elixir, which was always a delicious treat.

1½ tablespoons chia seeds
150 g/¾ cup light brown sugar
freshly squeezed juice of 7 limes
bunch of fresh mint, chopped
lime wheels, to garnish

SERVES 4–6

Rehydrate the chia seeds in 500 ml/2 cups water for at least 30 minutes.

Place the sugar in a jug/pitcher with 500 ml/2 cups water and stir until the sugar has dissolved. Add the chia seeds and any soaking water left, and the lime juice and mint and mix together. Serve in glasses with ice.

Note At my grandpa's house in Tlaxcala, we used to have a lima tree, a fruit more similar to bergamot. We would make a version of this water using them and the flavour was just amazing. So if you can find bergamot, I definitely recommend making a version with it.

Clockwise from left: Melon & Pecan Water, Tamarind Water and Lemon, Mint & Chia Water.

ROSEMARY & HIBISCUS WATER

AGUA DE JAMAICA CON ROMERO

This is one of the easiest and most popular *agua fresca served all over the country.*

70 g/1½ cups hibiscus flowers
150 g/¾ cup caster/superfine
  sugar, or to taste
4 fresh rosemary sprigs, to garnish

SERVES 6–8

Place the hibiscus flowers and the sugar in a saucepan with 500 ml/2 cups water, bring to the boil and cook for about 10 minutes. Remove from the heat and leave it to rest for about 30 minutes.

Strain the mixture into a jug/pitcher. Add another 500 ml/2 cups water and some ice and mix well. Serve in glasses with ice and a rosemary sprigs to garnish. Enjoy.

RICE & CINNAMON WATER

HORCHATA

This refreshing drink reminds me of hot evenings growing up in Tlaxcala when my mom used to make large quantities for all the family to enjoy.

170 g/1 cup white rice
  (basmati or similar)
1 cinnamon stick
200 g/1 cup caster/superfine
  sugar, or to taste
1 teaspoon vanilla extract
  (optional)

SERVES 8

Place the rice and cinnamon stick in a sealed jar or airtight container with 1 litre/4 cups water and leave overnight to soak. Make sure it is covered and left in a cool place.

The next day, discard the cinnamon stick and transfer the soaked rice to a blender and add the sugar and vanilla, if using. Blend until well combined and smooth. Pass the mixture through a fine-mesh sieve/strainer or pour it through muslin/cheesecloth into a bowl to strain. Transfer to a jug/pitcher filled with ice, top up with 1 litre/4 cups water and serve straight away.

Clockwise from left: Rosemary & Hibiscus Water and Rice & Cinnamon Water.

COCKTAILS
COCTELES

MARGARITA
MARGARITA

50 ml/1¾ fl oz. Arette Blanco
    tequila
25 ml/1 fl oz. Cointreau
25 ml/1 fl oz. fresh lime juice
lime wedge, to garnish
salt

SERVES 1

Prepare the rim of a coupe
glass with salt (see Note below).
Place all the ingredients in a
cocktail shaker filled with ice.
Secure the lid and hold the
shaker in both hands before
vigorously shaking in a horizontal
motion over your shoulder.
Shake for a slow count of ten.
Double strain the margarita into
the prepared glass and serve
with a lime wedge to garnish.

*Note To salt the rim a cocktail
glass, dampen the edge of the
glass with water or lime juice.
Tip some salt (or even some
Tajin seasoning) onto a saucer.
Turn the glass upside down and
press the edge of the glass into
the salt or seasoning to coat
the rim. Fill the glass with your
chosen cocktail.*

SPICY MARGARITA
MARGARITA PICANTE

Tajin seasoning
50 ml/1¾ fl oz. Arette Blanco
    tequila
25 ml/1 fl oz. Cointreau
25 ml/1 fl oz. fresh lime juice
25 ml/1 fl oz. sugar syrup
3 fresh jalapeño slices, plus extra
    to garnish

SERVES 1

Prepare the rim of a chilled
rocks glass (see Note below)
with Tajin seasoning. Place all
the remaining ingredients in
a cocktail shaker half-filled with
ice. Secure the lid and hold
the shaker in both hands before
vigorously shaking in a horizontal
motion over your shoulder.
Shake for a slow count of ten.
Strain the margarita into the
prepared glass and serve with
jalapeño slices to garnish.

CAVITA'S MARGARITA
MARGARITA DE CAVITA

3 chunks of fresh watermelon
40 ml/1½ fl oz. Arette Blanco
    tequila
10 ml/½ fl oz. Ojo De Dios
    Espadin mezcal
30 ml/1¼ fl oz. fresh lime juice
20 ml/1 fl oz. sugar syrup
1 teaspoon Tajin seasoning

SERVES 1

Muddle the watermelon chunks
in a cocktail shaker. Add the rest
of the ingredients and shake.
Double strain the margarita into
a rocks glass filled with ice.

SPICY MEZCALITA
MEZCALITA PICANTE

2 fresh jalapeño slices, plus extra
    to garnish
50 ml/1¾ fl oz. Ojo De Dios
    Espadin mezcal
20 ml/1 fl oz. Cointreau
20 ml/1 fl oz. sugar syrup
25 ml/1 fl oz. fresh lime juice
Tajin seasoning

SERVES 1

Prepare the rim of a chilled
rocks glass (see Note below)
with Tajin seasoning. Muddle
the jalapeño slices in a cocktail
shaker. Add the rest of the
ingredients and shake. Double
strain into the prepare glass.

HOT FRUIT PUNCH
PONCHE

This drink is very popular especially during Christmas. In Mexico we use little fruits call tejocotes that are like wild apples and add either tequila, mezcal or whisky for a wonderfully festive boozy punch.

1 cone of piloncillo
   (Mexican pure cane sugar) or
   200 g/1 cup dark brown sugar
1 cinnamon stick
25 g /½ cup hibiscus flowers
60 g /½ cup peeled tamarind
4 (15 cm/6 in.) sugar cane sticks,
   each cut into 6 pieces
100 g/1 cup chopped apple
   (Bramley or Golden Pippin
   are best)
100 g/1 cup chopped pear,
   cut into wedges
70 g/½ cup pitted/stoned prunes
6 guavas
tequila, mezcal or whisky, to taste
   (around 1 shot per cup)

SERVES 10

Place 2 litres/8 cups water, the piloncillo or sugar, cinnamon, hibiscus and tamarind in a large saucepan over a medium-high heat and cook for 15 minutes. Add the sugar cane and cook for a further 10 minutes. Add the fruit, bring back to the boil and simmer for 15 minutes. Transfer to a punch bowl, add a shot of your chosen alcohol to cups and top up with hot punch.

This page: Margarita and Spicy Margarita. Opposite: Cavita's Margarita and Spicy Mezcalita.

JALAPEÑO SOUR

JALAPEÑO AGRIA

Jalapeño sour has a very green, freshly cut herb taste. It makes a great welcome drink.

3 fresh jalapeño slices,
   plus extra to garnish
50 ml/1¾ fl oz. Arette Blanco
   tequila
25 ml/1 fl oz. agave syrup
25 ml/1 fl oz. egg white

SERVES 1

Place the jalapeño slices in a cocktail shaker (do not muddle in a delicate glass). Using a gentle muddling tool, press and twist lightly, do this two or three times. Add the rest of the ingredients to the shaker and add ice. Shake and serve in a chilled rocks glass. You can add extra jalapeño slices to garnish if you wish.

THE CALM

LA CALMA

This cocktail is very refreshing. Raicilla is an agave distilled in the north of the country.

50 ml/1¾ fl oz. Raicilla Mexicat
15 ml/¾ fl oz. Kwai Feh Lychee
   liqueur
20 ml/1 fl oz. Green Chartreuse
peeled lychee, to garnish

SERVES 1

Half-fill a mixing glass with ice. Add all the cocktail ingredients to the glass. Place a bar spoon inside the glass, hold it at the top of the twisted part, then gently rotate it around the inside edge of the glass for 15–20 rotations. Pour into a chilled rocks glass and serve garnished with a peeled lychee.

AZTEC MORNING

MAÑANA AZTECA

This is a good option to serve with dessert. Reduce the amount of agave syrup if you prefer a less sweet drink.

10 ml/2 teaspoons agave syrup
dulce de leche and desiccated
   coconut, to rim
25 ml/1 fl oz. Ojo de Dios
   Espadin mezcal
25 ml/1 fl oz. Ojo de Dios
   Cafe mezcal
25 ml/1 fl oz. Kalani coconut
   rum liqueur
50 ml/2 fl oz. espresso
edible cornflower, to garnish

SERVES 1

Prepare the rim of a chilled Martini glass (see page 162) using the dulce de leche and desiccated coconut. Place all the cocktail ingredients in a cocktail shaker half-filled with ice. Secure the lid and hold the shaker in both hands before vigorously shaking in a horizontal motion over your shoulder. Shake for a slow count of ten. Strain the cocktail into the prepared glass and garnish with an edible cornflower.

Clockwise from front: Jalapeno Sour, The Calm and Aztec Morning.

DOÑA LUCHA
DOÑA LUCHA

The Espadin mezcal gives this cocktail a special flavour, which pairs well with any Mexican dish.

50 ml/1¾ fl oz. Lost Explorer Espadin mezcal
10 ml/½ fl oz. Campari
20 ml/1 fl oz. St Germain elderflower liqueur
20 ml/1 fl oz. fresh lime juice
10 ml/½ fl oz. sugar syrup
edible flowers, to garnsh

SERVES 1

Place all the cocktail ingredients in a cocktail shaker half-filled with ice. Secure the lid and hold the shaker in both hands before vigorously shaking in a horizontal motion over your shoulder. Shake for a slow count of ten. Strain the cocktail into a chilled Doña Lucha glass and garnish with edible flower petals.

MAYAN NIGHTS
NOCHE MAYA

This is another cocktail that I serve with dessert or as digestif after a nice meal.

25 ml/1 fl oz. Bumbu Cream rum liqueur
25 ml/1 fl oz. Ojo de Dios Cafe mezcal
20 ml/1 fl oz. sugar syrup
25 ml/1 fl oz. rice milk
50 ml/1¾ fl oz. espresso
finely ground coffee, for dusting

SERVES 1

Place all the cocktail ingredients in a cocktail shaker filled with ice. Secure the lid and hold the shaker in both hands before vigorously shaking in a horizontal motion over your shoulder. Shake for a slow count of ten. Strain the cocktail into a chilled coupe glass and dust the surface of the drink with ground coffee.

CITLALI
CITLALI

The touch of corn makes this cocktail unique. Pox is a liquor made of corn, sugar cane and wheat, which is very important in Mayan culture as it has ceremonial uses.

50 ml/1¾ fl oz. Pox
10 ml/½ fl oz. agave syrup
5 dashes of Angostura bitters
charred baby corn, to garnish

SERVES 1

Place all the cocktail ingredients in a cocktail shaker filled with ice. Secure the lid and hold the shaker in both hands before vigorously shaking in a horizontal motion over your shoulder. Shake for a slow count of ten. Strain the cocktail into a chilled Nick & Nora glass and garnish with the baby corn.

Clockwise from left: Doña Lucha, Mayan Nights and Citlali.

HOT DRINKS
BEBIDAS CALIENTES

CHOCOLATE WITH MILK OR WATER

CHOCOLATE CON LECHE O AGUA

Chocolate has been very popular in Mexico since pre-Hispanic times – it was even used as a currency at one time. It would have been made with vanilla, flowers and honey at that time. When 16th-century settlers introduced cows to America, chocolate started to be mixed with milk. In Oaxaca, this chocolate drink is still served with water and you are often given a choice between water and milk when you order it. In the Mayan area, cacao is still used as a sacred drink or medicinal beverage.

1 litre/4 cups milk or water
350 g/12 oz. Oaxacan-style
  chocolate

SERVES 4–5

Place the milk or water in a saucepan over a medium-high heat and bring to the boil. Stir in the chocolate until melted. In Mexico, we use a *molinillo* (see page 189). Once, the chocolate is properly mixed, take it off the heat and try to make foam with the molinillo. If you don't have a molinillo, the same result can be achieved with a balloon whisk.

Note Mexican chocolate is usually freshly made in Mexico, so the aroma is very special. Some varieties are blended with spices like cloves, cinnamon or with other flavourings like almonds. This makes a very special tasting chocolate. I recommend the Mayordomo brand if you can find it.

POT COFFEE

CAFÉ DE OLLA

Usually this drink is prepared in a clay pot (olla), hence the name. In some regions, people also add cloves, orange or lime rind.

1 cone of piloncillo
  (Mexican pure cane sugar)
½ cinnamon stick (preferably
  Mexican cinnamon)
4 teaspoons freshly ground coffee
  (not too fine)

SERVES 4–5

Place the piloncillo and cinnamon in a saucepan with 1 litre/4 cups water over a medium–high heat. Bring to the boil, then add the ground coffee and turn off the heat. Let it rest for about 5 minutes – the coffee should settle at the bottom of the pot. Carefully ladle into cups and serve straight away.

Note It is always good to use a small fine-mesh sieve/strainer when you serve the coffee to avoid any little coffee grounds in the cups.

Clockwise from front: Chocolate with Water and Pot Coffee.

DESSERTS
POSTRES

CREME CARAMEL

FLAN

This is my Aunt Lupita's flan recipe. She is the oldest in my mom's family and likes to make this dessert whenever there are gatherings at her house. You can experiment with adding different flavours to this basic recipe, such as chocolate or coffee, to suit your tastes.

6 eggs
240 ml/1 cup condensed milk
240 ml/1 cup evaporated milk
240 ml/1 cup full-fat/whole milk
1 tablespoon vanilla extract
300 g/1½ cups caster/superfine
  sugar

six 8-cm/3-in. glass ramekins

SERVES 6

Preheat the oven to 180°C/160°C fan/350°F/Gas 4.

Place the eggs, all the milks and vanilla extract in a food processor or blender and blend together for about 1 minute.

Place the sugar in a saucepan with 2 tablespoons water. Shake the pan first to half dissolve the sugar in the water, then cook over a medium heat until you have an amber-coloured caramel.

Once the caramel is ready, pour about a tablespoon into each ramekin – use a metal spoon or pour directly from the saucepan if easier. Leave to cool completely, then pour the cream mixture on top until the ramekins are two-thirds full. Cover each ramekin with kitchen foil.

Place the ramekins in a large, deep roasting pan. Place the roasting pan in the middle of the oven and pour in warm water around the ramekins so that it comes to about half or two-thirds of the way up the sides of the ramekins. Bake in the preheated oven for about 40 minutes.

Test to see if they are cooked by piercing each flan with a knife; if it comes out clean, they are ready. Leave them to cool down, then transfer to the fridge until ready to serve.

VARIATION: *To make a Dulce de Leche Crème Caramel* (Flan de Cajeta) *Simply make as above but add 120 ml/½ cup dulce de leche to the food processor when mixing the ingredients. Cook as instructed following the main recipe, then cool and refrigerate until ready to serve.*

Note *The crème caramels can also be cooked on the hob. Place a small round metal rack the size of the saucepan into a large pan. Add water to cover the rack. Place the ramekins on the rack. Cover the pan with a lid or kitchen foil and place over a medium-high heat. Once the water starts to boil, lower the heat and simmer for about 40 minutes. Cool and refrigerate as before.*

SWEET FRITTERS
BUÑUELOS

In Mexico, this kind of sweet snack is usually found at a fair stall and is traditionally served with guava and piloncillo (cane sugar) syrup (see Note below). Some old-style bakeries used to make them as daily bread but without the syrup.

30 g/2 tablespoons butter, at room temperature
50 g/¼ cup caster/superfine sugar
300 g/2½ cups plain/all-purpose flour, plus extra for dusting
3 eggs
1 litre/4 cups vegetable oil

CINNAMON SUGAR
300 g/1½ cups caster/superfine sugar
30 g/2 tablespoons ground cinnamon

MAKES ABOUT 20 BUÑUELOS

Place the butter and sugar in a electric stand mixer and blend together until they are homogenized. Add the flour and mix until combined. Start to add the eggs, one at a time, mixing each one into the dough before adding the next. Work the dough until the gluten has been activated, the dough becomes elastic and looks smooth.

Dust the inside of a mixing bowl with flour. Place the dough in the bowl, sprinkle a bit more flour on top and cover with cling film/plastic wrap, making sure it doesn't touch the dough. Leave it to rest for about 1 hour.

Dust the work surface/counter top with some flour and make small balls from the dough, weighing about 15–20 g/¾ oz. each. Use a floured rolling pin to roll the balls into circles, rolling them as thinly as possible.

Heat the vegetable oil in a heavy-based saucepan to 170°C/325°F on a cooking thermometer. Deep fry the buñuelos for about 2–3 minutes until they are golden. Carefully remove them from the oil and place on kitchen paper to absorb any excess oil.

Mix the sugar and cinnamon together and sprinkle this all over the buñuelos while they are still hot. Preferably eat the buñuelos the same day, otherwise they could become soggy.

Note To make a guava and piloncillo syrup to serve with your buñuelos, simply place 240 ml/1 cup water, 200 g/1 cup piloncillo, molasses or dark brown sugar and 1 cinnamon stick in a saucepan and bring to the boil. Cook for about 3 minutes, stirring often, until the syrup has thickened. Add 250 g/9 oz. cubed guava and leave to cool before using.

CORN CAKE
PAN DE ELOTE

This cake is very well known all over Mexico. In the area where I grew up, Azcapotzalco in Mexico City, you can find them at the local bakery, where the bakers have a funny way of cooking them in recycled sardine cans. I think that makes them a very special preparation. Also, I will say that using native Mexican corn gives the best flavour, but it is not always easy to find outside of Mexico. Sweet yellow corn is usually easier to fine, which has a lower starch content, but with this recipe you will still get a really good result.

3 tablespoons nixtamalized white corn flour (see Note below) or gluten-free flour
10 g/2 teaspoons baking powder
130 g/⅔ cup caster/superfine sugar
540 g/2¼ cups fresh corn, at room temperature
30 ml/2 tablespoons full-fat/whole milk, at room temperature
3 large/US extra-large eggs
140 g/1¼ sticks unsalted butter, melted, plus extra for greasing

TO SERVE
vanilla ice cream
good-quality caramel sauce

20-cm/8-in. round cake pan

**MAKES 1 LARGE CAKE
(SERVES 6–8)**

Preheat the oven to 170°C/150°C fan/325°F/Gas 3 and grease the round cake pan.

Mix all the dry ingredients in a large bowl, then add to a food processor with the corn, milk and eggs and blend together. Continue mixing and gradually add the melted butter, a little at a time, until the mixture is very smooth.

Pour the cake mixture into the prepared cake pan and bake in the preheated oven for 45–60 minutes. To check if the cake is cooked, insert the tip of a knife or skewer in the centre; if it comes out clean, then the cake is cooked.

Leave the cake to cool in the pan for 20 minutes, then remove from the pan and leave to cool completely.

Serve warm with ice cream and caramel sauce. This cake tastes best when freshly made, but it will keep for up to 3 days in the fridge and can be reheated to serve.

Notes

I sometimes use frozen corn for this recipe, which works well as long as the corn is defrosted to room temperature, otherwise the mixture will separate if the corn is too cold.

Nixtamalized corn flour is made from corn that has been treated with lime, making it easier to digest. It can be bought online.

BANANA CAKE

PANQUE DE PLÁTANO

Mexico is super rich and abundant in fruits. Often households will have so much that they go off before they are able to eat them all. This is a lovely way to make use of bananas that are past their best.

115 g/1 stick unsalted butter, at room temperature, plus extra for greasing
3 over-ripe medium bananas (use 4 if they are small)
200 g/1 cup dark brown sugar
120 ml/½ cup light sour cream or Greek yogurt
2 eggs
1 tablespoon vanilla extract
1 teaspoon baking powder
170 g/1¼ cups plain/all-purpose flour
pinch of table salt
80 g/½ cup cacao nibs or chocolate chips

22 x 5 cm/8¾ x 2 in. loaf pan

MAKES 1 LOAF CAKE (SERVES 6–8)

Preheat the oven to 170°C/150°C fan/325°F/Gas 3. Grease the loaf pan.

Mash the bananas in a large bowl. Add the butter and sugar and mix until combined and smooth. Add the sour cream or Greek yogurt, eggs and vanilla extract and mix again until combined.

In another bowl, mix the baking powder, flour and salt, then fold this into the wet mixture. Don't over mix. Fold the cacao nibs or chocolate chips in last, reserving a handful to sprinkle on top once in the pan.

Pour the mixture into the prepared loaf pan, sprinkle with the reserved cacao nibs or chocolate chips and bake in the preheated oven for about 45–60 minutes. Check if it is cooked by piercing the centre of the cake with a skewer or tip of a knife; if it comes out clean, it's ready.

Leave the cake to cool down in the pan for at least 30 minutes before removing from the pan and serving in slices.

Note You can serve this delicious cake with chocolate or vanilla ice cream if liked.

MEXICAN RICE PUDDING
ARROZ CON LECHE

This is the simplest but tastiest recipe for rice pudding in Mexico.

180 g/1 cup pudding or short-grain
  rice, rinsed
480 ml/2 cups full-fat/whole milk
1 small cinnamon stick
1 tablespoon vanilla extract
1 whole clove
65 g/⅓ cup caster/superfine sugar
ground cinnamon, for sprinkling
sea salt

SERVES 2–3

Place the rice and 480 ml/2 cups water in a saucepan over a high heat and add a pinch of salt. Bring to the boil, then simmer for about 15–20 minutes until the rice is cooked.

Meanwhile, place the milk, cinnamon stick, vanilla, clove and sugar in a separate saucepan and bring to the boil. Once boiling, turn off the heat and cover the pan with a lid. Leave it to rest for at least 5 minutes, then strain. Add to the pan of rice and mix together.

Transfer the rice pudding to a bowl and cover with cling film/plastic wrap. Leave it to cool, then chill in the fridge for at least 2 hours before serving with a dusting of cinnamon on top.

Note *I love to add some finely chopped mixed nuts on top; other people like to add raisins.*

PINEAPPLE TAMALES

TAMALES DE PIÑA

**This is one of the most popular sweet tamales that you can find
at most tamal stalls in Central Mexico – a very popular flavour.**

200 g/1¾ sticks unsalted butter,
  at room temperature
250 g/1¼ cups caster/superfine
  sugar
500 g/3¾ cups tamal flour
  (see Note below)
240 ml/1 cup pineapple juice
1 tablespoon baking powder
200 g/1⅓ cups canned pineapple
  chunks in syrup or homemade
  pineapple compote
  (see Note below)
20 dry corn husks (leaves), soaked
  in warm water for 1 hour

MAKES ABOUT 12 TAMALES

Mix the butter and sugar in a food processor or stand mixer fitted
with the paddle attachment. Beat for 8 minutes, then add the tamal
flour and mix again, then add the pineapple juice. Keep mixing for
10 minutes. Add the baking powder and mix for another minute.
Mix in the pineapple chunks by hand until just folded through.

Remove the corn husks from the water and let them dry off for
a few minutes.

Follow the instructions on page 102 to prepare the tamales topping
the corn husks with about 60 g/2 oz. of the sweetened dough before
folding. Repeat until all the tamales have been prepared.

Preheat a steamer (*tamalera*). Add all the tamales, standing upright
in the steamer, with the open end facing up. Top with any spare
corn husks that you have and leave to steam for 60 minutes over
a medium heat. Serve straight away. I sometimes serve these tamales
with any leftover pineapple as well.

VARIATION: To make Chocolate Tamales (Tamales de Chocolate)
*Prepare the sweetened tamal dough as above but use 200 g/
1 cup caster/superfine sugar and 240 ml/1 cup full-fat/whole milk
instead of the pineapple juice, then add 200 g/7 oz. melted 70%
dark/bittersweet chocolate to make a chocolate dough. Mix in
3 tablespoons cacao nibs instead of the cubed pineapple at the end.
Continue preparing and steaming the tamales as instructed above.*

Notes
Tamal flour can be found online – look for harina para tamal *in online
Mexican food stores.*

*I like to make my own pineapple compote to add to the sweetened
tamal dough. Simply place the flesh from 1 pineapple, cut into small
cubes, with 300 g/1½ cups caster/superfine sugar and 240 ml/1 cup
water in a saucepan. Bring to the boil and cook until the water has
evaporated and the pineapple has caramelized slightly.*

SPICED CHOCOLATE MOUSSE

MOUSSE DE CHOCOLATE ESPECIADO

I love this recipe on a summer evening with a nice cup of tea. It can also be made for special gatherings with friends as it is easy to prepare ahead.

5 egg yolks
2 eggs
100 g/½ cup caster/superfine
   sugar
150 g/5½ oz. 70% dark/
   bittersweet chocolate
150 g/5½ oz. Mexican chocolate
300 g/1¼ cups double/heavy
   cream
½ tablespoon ground cinnamon
mixed berries and mint leaves,
   to serve

SERVES 6

Place the egg yolks and eggs in an electric stand mixer and whisk until light and foamy.

Place the sugar and 50 ml/scant ¼ cup water in a small saucepan over a medium-high heat. Heat to 117°C/242°F on a sugar/candy thermometer, then take off the heat.

Slowly add the sugar mixture to the eggs without stopping the mixer to make a pâté à bombe.

Place the chocolate in a microwave-safe bowl and heat it in the microwave in 10-second bursts until melted. Mix the cream and cinnamon into the chocolate, then gradually add the pâté à bombe.

Transfer the mousse to serving bowls or glasses. Leave to set in the fridge for about 3 hours before serving topped with some mixed berries and a mint leaf.

PECAN NUT LITTLE HORN COOKIES

CUERNITOS DE NUEZ

This is a traditional cookie that I remember from my childhood in Mexico City, which we used to find in the local bakeries.

200 g/1¾ sticks butter, at room temperature
70 g/½ cup icing/confectioner's sugar
1 tablespoon vanilla extract
50 g/½ cup ground pecan nuts
170 g/1¼ cups plain/all-purpose flour

TO FINISH
2 tablespoons icing/confectioner's sugar

baking sheet lined with parchment paper or silicone mat

MAKES ABOUT 40–50 BITE-SIZED COOKIES

Preheat the oven to 200°C/180°C fan/400°F/Gas 6.

Mix the butter, sugar and vanilla in an electric mixer until creamy.

Mix the ground pecan nuts and flour in a bowl. Add this to the butter mixture and mix to combine. Do not overwork the mixture. Leave it to rest in the fridge for about 40 minutes.

Take walnut-sized balls of the cookie dough and shape each one into little horn shapes. Place them on the lined baking sheet.

Bake the cookies in the preheated oven for about 12 minutes. Leave to cool, then dust with icing sugar. The cookies will keep in an airtight container for up to 1 week. Enjoy them with a morning coffee.

Note *Alternatively, you can dip half of each cookie in melted dark/bittersweet chocolate and leave to set.*

GLOSSARY

ACITRON A traditional sweet made from cactus that grows in desert areas in Mexico, although it can no longer be made this way due to the cactus being in danger of extinction.

ADOBO A chilli/chile paste, usually made from dried chillies/chiles and mixed spices.

AGAVE (OR MAGUEY) Known as the 'plant of one thousand uses', it is a plant with over 200 different species many of which are only found in Mexico.

AGUACHILE A basic mix of chilli/chile and water used to prepare one of the most famous dishes in Sinaloa – a type of ceviche with fresh prawns/shrimp, red onion and cucumber.

ASADA/ASADO/ASADOS To 'asar' means to cook something over charcoal. When an ingredient is described as asada (usually vegetables like tomatillos and onions), it should be cooked over hot coals or in a hot pan over a high heat until the skin has charred all over and the vegetable is soft and cooked. Traditionally this is done on top of the coals/embers of a fire. Alternatively, you can achieve the same results in a hot dry frying pan/skillet or comal or in an oven preheated to 200°C/180°C fan/400°F/ Gas 6 for 15 minutes.

AVOCADO LEAVES The leaves of the avocado tree are similar to anise in flavour. They are used mostly in the central and southern parts of Mexico, fresh or dried and blended into a powder.

AXIOTE/ACHIOTE A jungle red seed, used mainly in the Yucatán peninsula. It has a very unique flavour and can be bought as a paste from any good spice and wholefood stores or online.

BANANA LEAVES They are used to wrap different types of meat and fish to protect them while cooking, and also to wrap tamales.

BARBACOA A specific preparation with lamb or young goat. The meat is cooked under the soil in a type of natural underground oven, typical in central and some southern parts of Mexico.

CHAYOTE A type of sweet courgette/zucchini with little spikes on the skin. From the family of the cucurbitaceous.

CHICHARRON A crispy pork skin, similar to pork crackling.

CHOCHOYOTES They are little corn dough balls with a little hole in the middle used to give texture to recipes, but can also be used to thicken soups or broths.

COMAL An ancient Mexican kitchen utensil. It is a semi flat, round pan made out of clay, where made most of the basic recipes (tortillas, tostadas, soups, quesadillas, etc.) are made, but it is also a very useful utensil for toasting vegetables, seeds and chillies/ chiles when making sauces and moles.

CORN LEAVES There are two types: the leaves from the corn (the corn husk) and the leaves from the actual corn plant (the long ones). Both are used to prepare tamales.

ELOTE Is a fresh corn or 'young corn'. The root of this word from the Nahuatl *elotl*. Around 68 names exist for it in Mexico that corresponds to each different language.

EPAZOTE A Mexican native herb. It was very popular before the Spanish arrived and is now popular in other countries in America due to its unique flavour.

ESCABECHE A method of preserving an ingredient in vinegar.

HOJA SANTA POWDER Hoja santa (Piper auritum) is a plant that can be used either as medicine or in cooking.

HORCHATA A flavoured water drink, made with rice and sometimes with oats or nuts.

HUITLACHOCHE A fungus that grows on the corn plant that happens when water gets trapped inside the plant as it grows. It is very popular in Mexico.

MASA Corn dough.

MEXICAN CHOCOLATE This spiced chocolate unique to Mexico is made by the cacao bean paste being mixed with spices, usually cinnamon. Sugar and other flavourings, such as almonds can also be added.

MEXICAN OREGANO Oregano that grows in Mexico has a different aroma and taste.

MEZCAL From the Nahuatl *mezcalli, which* means 'cook agave', it is a Mexican spirit with DO, made from 12 to 15 different agave plants.

MOLCAJETE A traditional Mesoamerican mortar, made out of volcanic rocks. Used in the same way as a mortar and pestle.

MOLE From the Nahuatl *molli*, it means sauce. Moles can range from being very simple like guacamole, to very complex like Mole negro from Oaxaca or Poblano from Puebla with more than 20 ingredients.

MOLINILLO From the Nahuatl *moliniani*, meaning 'mix' or 'beat'. It is a round wooden kitchen tool with holes in it used to make a foam when making the hot Mexican chocolate drink.

NIXTAMAL The process of cooking corn kernels in water and calcium hydroxide (lime) to soften the corn, take out the kernels and make it more nutritious and easier to digest.

NIXTAMALIZED CORN FLOUR Made from nixtamal (corn that has been treated with lime), making it easier to digest. It can be bought online.

PILONCILLO A raw form of cane sugar widely used in Mexico. Molasses can be used as a substitute.

PUMPKIN FLOWERS The flowers from the pumpkin plant that are commonly used in Mexico. You can substitute any flowers from squash plants, including courgette flowers if you struggle to find them.

QUESILLO Also known as Oaxaca cheese and similar to mozzarella, but a bit saltier.

QUESO FRESCO A white, unpasteurized cheese. Most are soft in texture and flavour and add a fresh taste to any dish. Feta cheese is a good substitute.

TAMALES A Mexican dish made with corn dough, meat, veggies and sauce, cooked inside banana or corn leaves. There are many different variations of flavours and textures that can be used.

TATAMADOS *See Asada/asado/asadamos.*

TOMATILLOS A green round, acidic fruit from the physalis family. Originally from America, it is very popular for using in sauces.

TORTILLA A flat flexible type of 'bread' made from corn dough.

TOSTADA Made by frying tortillas or drying the tortillas In the oven or over the comal.

TOTOPOS Tortillas that have been cut into triangles and then deep-fried until crispy.

XOCONOSTLE A type of pickling pear, that is quite hard, acidic and sour. Comes from the Nahuatl *xococ*, meaning 'sour'.

TYPES OF CHILLIES

There are more than 100 different varieties of chilli/chile in Mexico. Here are just a few of my favourites.

ANCHO This is the name for a dried poblano chilli. It is often used with other chillies due to its low spice.

CASCABEL Named after the noise it makes when you shake the chilli, like a rattle. *Casacabel o sonaja* means 'rattle' in Spanish.

CHIPOTLE A type of dried smoky chilli.

HABANERO Most commonly used in the south of the country, especially in the Yucatán peninsula. It is most appreciated for its aroma and spiciness.

GUAJILLO One of the most common chillies due to his flavour. It's not particularly spicy so is often mixed with other chillies to increase spice levels.

GUERO A yellow chilli that comes in many shapes and sizes. They are not usually very spicy, but when pickled they add a fresh taste to a dish.

JALAPEÑO A very common fresh chilli now popular all over the world. Other similar fresh chillies used in Mexico are the chile de arbol or serrano that brings flavour to the Mexican sauces.

MORITA A dried chilli with very tense skin and purple tones. Often favoured for it's smoky flavour.

PASILLA This is the name for the dried version of the chilaca chilli (a large fresh green chilli). It has a very nice taste, with a prune-like sweetness to it.

POBLANO A large fresh chilli, commonly stuffed and cooked.

INDEX

ACKNOWLEDGEMENTS

It has been an amazing journey working on this book. I want to say a big thanks to the Ryland Peters & Small team – Leslie, Abi, Julia, Megan and all – for your guidance, hard work and patience. I never imagined that the process behind making a book could be so beautiful. It has been an intense journey, with lots of learning for me. To Annuska, for all your help – I felt a deep connection and understanding about Mexican culture as we worked.

Massive thanks to all those that have always had trust in me. Of course, first and foremost to my mother Helena and my sister Joss (mama Jocelyn) who have been there for me unconditionally and support me in all my unusual ideas.

Basit, Ana Lucia, Ernesto, Nicola – I can't imagine this journey without you, you mean a lot to me. A 'million thousand' thanks for being there for me, for your trust, your passion, your friendship, care and all the support that I have felt since the day we met. You rock! I love you all!

Thank you Mexico, for all the inspiration, the diversity, multicultural beauty, such a colourful country and I will always carry you deeply in my heart. Thank you to the native cultures and *cocineras/cocineros tradicionales* for your resiliency and commitment to your ancestral traditions; for your love to this land and for preserving the seeds and nature for the future generations. Thank you to all those people keeping recipes alive and teaching with love and respect.

I love this verse that our ancestors used to say: *Dejemos al menos flores, dejemos al menos cantos.* 'Let's leave at least flowers and songs'. For me this means that the knowledge of a culture and its biodiversity is the most important heritage we can leave/share/keep for this world. I hope that many more generations will keep cooking and enjoying these flavours as much as I do.

And thank you to the readers! I hope you enjoy cooking these recipes and learn a bit more about my Mexico. It will be great to see you celebrating Mexican flavours with your friends and family! *Viva la Cocina Mexicana!*

PICTURE CREDITS

All commissioned photography is copyright Ryland Peters & Small 2023, except for:

© Adriana Cavita 2023
Pages 5 top right, top left, bottom left; 37 top right, top left, middle right, bottom right; 51 all; 85 top right, top left, middle right; 113 top left; 137 top left, bottom left; 153 top left, bottom left.

© Lucy Richards 2023
Pages 7, 13, 27 all, 28, 113 top right, middle right, bottom right.

© Oliver Villegas 2023
Back cover.

© Adobe Stock Images
Page 37 middle right, Daniel; 85 middle left, Liliana; 137 top right, Carlos Neri.

The artworks featured on pages 35, 89 and 151 are murals created by the wonderful Iván Salamanca for my restaurant in London. More of his work can be seen on Instagram @ivandsalamanca.